CW01433287

HEARTBEATS

HEARTBEATS

BJÖRN BORG

[signature]

Signed by the Author

BJÖRN BORG

HEARTBEATS

A Memoir

As told to Patricia Borg

Translated by Bradley Harmon

SPHERE

SPHERE

First published in Great Britain in 2025 by Sphere

1 3 5 7 9 10 8 6 4 2

Hjärtslag © Patricia Borg, first published by Norstedts, Sweden, in 2025.
Published by agreement with Norstedts Agency.
Translated by Bradley Harmon

The moral right of the author has been asserted.

All rights reserved.
No part of this publication may be reproduced, stored in a
retrieval system, or transmitted, in any form or by any means, without
the prior permission in writing of the publisher, nor be otherwise circulated
in any form of binding or cover other than that in which it is published
and without a similar condition including this condition being
imposed on the subsequent purchaser.

A CIP catalogue record for this book
is available from the British Library.

Hardback ISBN 978-1-4087-2231-2
Trade paperback ISBN 978-1-4087-2232-9

Typeset in Caslon by M Rules
Printed and bound in Great Britain by
Clays Ltd, Elcograf S.p.A

Papers used by Sphere are from well-managed forests
and other responsible sources.

FSC
MIX
Paper | Supporting
responsible forestry
www.fsc.org   FSC® C104740

Sphere
An imprint of
Little, Brown Book Group
Carmelite House
50 Victoria Embankment
London EC4Y 0DZ

The authorised representative
in the EEA is
Hachette Ireland
8 Castlecourt Centre
Dublin 15, D15 XTP3, Ireland
(email: info@hbgi.ie)

An Hachette UK Company
www.hachette.co.uk

www.littlebrown.co.uk

Contents

Part V: Game, Set, Match (2000–2025)

Prologue

Thump-thump, thump-thump, thump-thump ...
The sound of a heart beating, or a ball bouncing.
It's probably what most people associate thumping
with. In my case it's neither of these. For me
there's just silence.

It's the middle of the '90s. I'm in a small city in Holland and I've just started playing tennis again. The senior tour has reinstilled the joy of the game in me and this time my dad is with me on the road, just like many times before. Dad, his hair combed back and held in place with a huge amount of Brylcreem like always, is both my biggest fan and my closest friend. It means a lot that he still wants to come along with me.

We'll have to go to the tennis stadium soon, where I'll play in the final of a senior competition. The sun is shining, and the entire week has been perfectly planned out, but last night everything went wrong. It started out well with a lovely dinner with Dad and all my tennis buddies, but something in my head snapped – something that was not uncommon with me. There was too much of everything. Alcohol, drugs, pills – my preferred ways of self-medication when I start to feel bad in these sorts of situations. When Dad comes to pick me up, the only thing I can mutter is a meagre 'I won't be able to play today. I feel too horrible.'

He brushes off my objections and assures me that everything will be fine. Deep down he probably hopes that everything will sort itself out, that I'll pull myself together like I have before.

We start walking and I feel the ground swaying under my feet. It's like I'm hovering in place, I can't move forward. We have to walk over a bridge, one of those typical Dutch bridges over a canal where the houseboats bob up and down, moored with thick ropes. That's when I sink to the ground. Everything goes black and the unthinkable happens. I'm dying.

I can't see the tunnel with light at the end nor any life flashing by, everything's just gone. My heart is no longer going *thump-thump*, because it's stopped. But before it goes black I have enough time to think: How did things end up like this?

As luck would have it, there are people around us who manage to save my life. Dad is probably standing there, hands in the pockets of his trousers, outwardly wearing a mask of unconcern but inwardly paralysed by fear. It's how he used to react, terrified of confrontation and in that situation probably not a man of action.

I survived and that was fortunate, because I love life and today I'm so grateful that it didn't all end in that moment. It's said that a heart beats 2.5 billion times in a life. Mine has beaten a few less, and it's not because of my slow pulse.

After the collapse on the bridge I knew that I was about to play my most important match ever. The match against myself – the most stubborn of all opponents – and against the drugs. I was born under the sign of Gemini and I've always felt that I've had two personalities within me, kind of like Dr Jekyll and Mr Hyde. A little devil that sits on my shoulder and persistently tries to drag me down into a suffocating darkness.

That fateful day in Holland was the closest he came to succeeding.

PART ONE

A Family Affair (1956–1974)

1

It Was the Three
of Us. Always

My first memory is of a police station. I was three years old and tears were running down my cheeks. My stomach was aching from fear and worry, the room was cold and sterile and there was a constant buzzing sound. I thought of Mum, who always said that if I didn't behave the police would come and get me. Now that had happened and I was trembling in fear. Why had I ended up here, why had I been so stupid?

A few minutes later, Mum came and got me and I understood that it wasn't my fault. I had just gotten separated from her and gotten lost.

My family has always meant the world to me. I was born on Wednesday, 6 June 1956 and as the first child I was eagerly awaited. At that time, we lived in the seaside town of Nynäshamn, but very soon after we moved to the beautiful industrial city of Södertälje just south of Stockholm. It was the 1960s and the city was dominated by the commercial vehicle company Scania and the ice hockey team Södertälje SK. The Social Democrats governed the municipality, just as they did in all of Sweden.

We lived in a two-bedroom apartment in a normal green building on Torekällgatan. Attached to the building was a row of garages whose doors were perfect for a ball-crazy kid who didn't have any friends to play with. All around there were both trees and small side streets. It was just me, my mum Margareta and my dad Rune. From the very beginning we were a close-knit family – we did everything together. Neither Mum nor Dad had siblings, and because Dad had a complicated relationship with his own family, we hardly ever saw them. On the other hand, I was very close to my grandparents on my mother's side and we would always spend time with them. They didn't have any other friends, from what I remember, and nor did my parents.

I know that they tried to have more children, but unfortunately without any success. My mum eventually had to have her ovaries removed due to the strain of failed pregnancies. So I remained an only child. It was a great sadness for my parents and something that certainly contributed to us three being such a strong unit. It was the three of us. Always. A tight family with my mum Margareta at the helm.

My dream of being a sports star came early. Perhaps because my nursery school was in an area called Badparken. It's an historic park that had several tennis courts in the summer and an ice rink in the winter. Mum and I would walk past Badparken every day on the way to nursery and I couldn't pull my eyes away from all the kids playing different games and sports.

Perhaps I have Badparken and all the people who played sports there to thank for the fact that I got to play both tennis and ice hockey during primary school. I first played ice hockey with a team called the Seagulls, which was a very good association where you learned the basics of both skating and technique. My father Rune and another parent then started their own hockey team, SAIF, so that we children would have a team to play and train with. It was a real passion project that made it possible for all children to play, alongside the city's more elite hockey teams. It was clearly for fun, but for me it quickly became serious.

I rapidly developed as a player and when a request came from the 'real' club Södertälje SK to play on their boys' team, it blew my mind, because that's exactly what I'd wanted. They played in the highest series and I put everything into it, gave as much as I could. The reward came in the big youth tournament St Erik's Cup, when our team made it all the way to the final. But for me personally, the highlight was when I was named player of the match in both the quarter- and semi-finals. I think I was already beginning to feel that individual sports appealed to me more.

Starting school is a big deal for every child, and it was for me too, though it took a little while before I found my place in the class. When I started elementary school at Blombacka School, my mum came with me. I remember feeling nervous and a bit scared, even though I'd already played with some of the kids who were starting in the same class.

I know I was a fairly happy kid. The only thing I found really tough during those years was that Mum worked as a childminder so we could make ends meet. On weekdays, I never got any peace and quiet at home with all the daycare kids running around. I couldn't even be alone in my room, I was constantly being interrupted.

My room was a typical boy's room, with posters from the

Buster comic and sea-grass-patterned wallpaper where the occasional booger would end up stuck. Everything I needed was in there: my bed, a few shelves, and a desk by the window that looked out over the parking lot. Right below was the garage door. I loved my little nest, I could lie there and read comic books and let my mind wander. Sometimes I got so lost in them I barely heard what anyone was saying to me.

My room was cosy and comforting, but I wanted it to myself. I didn't want to share it. Every kid probably needs some time alone now and then, but with all those other kids around, that was hard for me. Luckily, I had my sports to focus on.

Mum had high expectations for me when it came to school and everything around it. I remember once in middle school when she got furious with me. It was the end-of-year ceremony, and for the occasion she'd dressed me in new, stylish white clothes. Of course, I'd figured out there were shortcuts on the school grounds, and one of them went down a grassy slope. I was running a bit late to the ceremony and took the shortcut, and of course I slipped in my nice clothes. When Mum saw me, she assumed I'd rolled around in the grass on purpose rather than accidentally falling and gave me one of her angriest scoldings. She could really get mad and wasn't shy about showing it. Dad, on the other hand, rarely lost his temper, so I guess they balanced each other out that way, like in so many other ways.

During secondary school, I was pretty annoyed when I didn't get the top grade in P.E. because the teacher didn't think I was good enough at rhythm and dance. Sadly, he was probably right because I didn't like those kinds of 'sports', so it went the way it went. But I almost always did my homework and kept up with school, mostly because it was safer that way, otherwise Mum would be on my case. And I ended up with good grades.

Both Mum and Grandma Greta had this idea that I should become a priest when I grew up. Dad didn't agree at all, he would've much preferred I pursue a career in sports. To this day, I have no idea where Mum and Grandma got the priest idea from. No one in our family had ever been particularly religious. But we've always had a spiritual side, the kind where you might feel the presence of the dead, sense energies in houses, or have premonitions about things that are going to happen. But I didn't think much about that back then, it was something I only came to understand much later in life.

Eventually, Mum and Grandma dropped the priest thing, and that was fine, because everyone in our family was so into sports. Early on, everything we did together revolved around hockey, table tennis, football, and tennis. Back then, there wasn't 24/7 sports on TV like there is now. Mostly it was just football, especially on Saturdays, and Dad and I never missed it. Watching English league football was a given. We'd sit there with our carefully planned betting slips and get super excited to see if we'd win big, which of course we never did.

Our family had supported Charlton Athletic ever since my grandfather's days, not exactly the hottest team to follow now, since they seem to drop a division every year. But that doesn't matter, I'll always be loyal to them. In Sweden, my team was Hammarby IF for football, and of course Södertälje SK for ice hockey. Once you've chosen a team, you stick with them for life, at least that's how I see it.

Early on, I developed a special Sunday ritual. I honestly don't know how it started, but every Sunday evening I'd take a long bath. Weekends were usually packed with sports, and I loved sinking into the hot water and letting my thoughts just dissolve. I could lie there for ages, thinking about absolutely nothing.

Even when the water cooled and my fingers turned wrinkly, it was the best way to relax.

Mum had her routine too, every night she'd lay out the clothes I was supposed to wear to school the next day. They'd be neatly folded on a chair next to the bed, and I'd look at them thinking, 'No way am I wearing that'.

The worst was when there was a turtleneck. It was itchy and full of static, and when I put it on my hair would stand on end. Not being allowed to choose my own clothes was something I really hated. But Mum was the one who decided those things, that's just how it was.

Still, I usually looked forward to going to school. I was naturally an early riser, and the moment Mum woke me up, I'd jump out of bed and get ready. It was fun seeing my friends again, especially after a weekend apart.

All in all, my school years were pretty carefree. But of course, I have some painful memories too. One was my severe underbite, which both the doctors and my parents were determined to fix. Every night, I had to wear a special dental device that stretched my jaw to correct the bite. It had a thick elastic band that pulled my chin back, and it really hurt because it was so tight around my head. I wore it for a whole year, probably, but thankfully it worked and I have no problems with my bite today. It was worth the effort, but I still remember that time as incredibly tough, especially when I was invited for sleepovers, which I rarely wanted to do because of that awful brace.

My family's close bond might seem a bit unusual, but I've always felt secure in myself, and I think that comes from that sense of belonging. Dad was the rock of the family. I loved tagging along with him whenever I could, especially to table tennis tournaments he was competing in. He was really good at table tennis,

I probably inherited my ball sense from him. Even today, I still play now and then, it's fun and it reminds me of all those great times with Dad.

One of those moments was the spark that made me a tennis player. I was maybe eight or nine when I went with him to a tournament. Before it started, they announced that the winner would get to choose their own prize. One of the prizes was a tennis racket. I wanted it so badly and begged Dad to pick it if he won. Being the kind soul he was, he did just that, first he won, then he chose the racket.

Who knows what would've happened if I hadn't gone with him that day to the Bålsta Championships? Was it fate, or some higher power guiding me? No one can say for sure. But that was the day tennis really entered my life. For the first time, I had a tennis racket of my own. Until then, I'd just watched wide-eyed as the other kids played in Badparken.

The racket was way too heavy for me, so I had to use both hands for both backhand and forehand. You could say that's when I developed my unusual playing style.

Later, my coaches tried to get me to let go of my left hand and change my grip. But I didn't care what they said, I just played the way that felt right to me. That's how I ended up with a two-handed backhand. I eventually gave up the two-handed forehand, though, reluctantly. But that wasn't until much later, when Percy Rosberg became my first professional coach. I never did give up the two-handed backhand, and after me, a lot of players started using it too.

I became a true all-round athlete early on, mostly because I played both hockey and tennis, especially in the winters. We played tennis indoors in a sports hall with a classic hard plastic floor, with lines painted for all kinds of sports. The surface was incredibly fast. In summer, it was all about clay courts in Badparken. I don't remember there being a tennis school for kids, but I hung out there from morning to night in case anyone wanted to play. This split between indoor and outdoor seasons forced me to learn to adapt to different speeds and surfaces, and that gave me a big advantage when I went pro later.

Every day after school, my tennis racket or skates would be waiting for me in the hallway. I'd grab whatever I needed and head straight for Badparken. In summer it was the tennis courts; in winter I'd kick off the skate guards and glide onto the ice. I was actually a Cub Scout too, but mostly because I wanted to collect as many badges as I could. I was competitive early on.

If the courts were open, I'd practise serving. If they were full, I'd stay anyway, watching and learning from the others. I was there constantly, before and after school, all weekend, and of course every school break.

Often a spot would open up because someone didn't show, and sometimes someone scheduled for doubles got sick, and I was always ready to jump in. I looked up to the older junior players, they were so good and hit the ball so hard. For me as a little kid, getting to play with them was incredibly educational, even if they didn't always think it was fun to play with me, even though I was good for my age.

As tennis was becoming more important to me, my parents bought a small neighbourhood grocery store on Torekällgatan. It was one of those old-school food shops that sold just about everything. After school, it felt special to walk in there and grab a little treat for myself or a friend. The shop had everything, except fresh fish, and it quickly became a hangout for everyone in the area. But it also took up a lot of my parents' time. They were never really off work. Deliveries had to be received, customers had to be helped, long opening hours kept, and everything had to be clean and tidy.

So my world back then revolved around four main things: the shop, school, Badparken and the sports hall. The hub for all of it was our apartment building on Torekällgatan, I was close to everything. And that's where I found my best training partner – one of the garage doors on our block.

I was always at that garage door. Even after dark there was still enough light from nearby streetlights to keep playing. I'd stand there practicing my shots, forehand and backhand, much to the neighbours' annoyance. At first, the ones living closest complained, but after I promised to play only at certain times, things settled down.

That garage door has been written about a lot, but what people don't always know is that I was just as obsessed with hockey during those years. I practised shooting pucks at that same garage too. Once I got the idea to see how many times I could hit the brick wall above the basement windows. That worked for a while, until there was a loud 'pang' and a window shattered. I had to pay for it myself, and that stung.

After that, tennis felt like the safer bet. My scoring system was simple: I had to hit the same spot on the garage door five times in a row, if I missed, the 'point' went to my imaginary opponent. In my head, I was in the Wimbledon final or a decisive Davis Cup match. Those were the tournaments I dreamed about when I stood there in the evenings, practicing my strokes. I wasn't just going to be the best tennis player in the world, I was going to be the greatest of all time.

2

Out Into the World

When I was eleven years old, I played in my first junior championship. In the pictures from that tournament, I look small and frail, with short hair parted to the side and dressed in a white tennis undershirt typical of that time. It wasn't unsurprising that I looked so small, because there was only one age bracket and most of my opponents were a year or even two years older than me. As I remember it, there were a few players selected from each part of the country. There weren't as many teenagers playing tennis back then, so although the competition was steep, it wasn't nearly as fierce as it is today.

The matches were played in the fantastic tennis pavilion in Östermalm, one of Stockholm's more affluent neighbourhoods. *Kråkslottet*, or the Crow Castle, as it's called today, was built at the end of the nineteenth century and had a wooden floor that was even faster than the plastic floor at home in Södertälje. Most people felt both a little queasy and intimidated when they stepped onto the historic court. But for me there was only one feeling: I wanted to win.

I lost in two sets in a row – 6–0, 6–0 – and ended up going home sad and pissed off. Even then I realised that in order to win the most important thing was to train. So training itself became a priority for me early on. During my active tennis career, I played at least four hours a day, in addition to running, skipping rope, and using my body weight to do, for example, sit-ups and push-ups, all to make it as strong as possible. However, I never trained in a gym or lifted weights.

I would often run several miles, but I also started early on with doing fast and explosive intervals, which was what was needed on a tennis court. I was one of the first to spend time running beyond the tennis court and my distances ranged from 100 metres to 10,000 metres, with times that stood up well to the Swedish competition. When I ran 60 metres, no one beat me in the first ten metres, which are the most important steps on a tennis court, and I know I could've won the 10,000-metre race if I'd wanted to. I was both explosive and had endurance, and I'm not exaggerating when I say that I never felt the least bit tired on a tennis court.

The losses in my first real tennis tournament stung, but the great thing about most sports is that there will always be more competitions and new championships. The next stop was the regional championships in Katrineholm – a small town about 150 kilometres south-west of Stockholm – where I won my first tournament. I remember so well how proud I was when I got home, I even rang the doorbell so that my mum had to come and open it. And there I was: with a big smile and a trophy. I think my mum was both proud and moved when she saw that I was being rewarded for all my training. She knew that I had put my whole soul into it.

My family has always been the centre of my life, it was that way then and it's that way now. When I was younger, my parents worked so much in the shop that I often had to stay at home with my grandparents. My grandfather Martin always drove me to and from practice, even though he worked full time at Ericsson and rarely had days off or holidays. They spent summers on Resarö, a small island in the Stockholm archipelago outside Vaxholm, and the lived the rest of the year in Fruängen, a suburb south-west of central Stockholm. One of my earliest memories is of me running around Resarö, running and running and my grandmother chasing after me. She always said that I had so much energy to burn. Sometimes she would simply grab a rope and tie it round my stomach and then to a tree. Then I could only get so far, so there was no risk of me running off and getting hurt. I suppose she also needed some rest between laps.

When I was a child, Resarö was an idyllic summer island. Nowadays, many people live there permanently, despite the island being so small. Because it's an island, it was natural to spend a lot of time out on the sea; we would fish, go boating, row, bathe and swim, and sometimes my grandfather and I would go to Vaxholm to buy ice cream. It was the kind of upbringing that many Swedish children were treated to. There is also something special about the Swedish summer in the archipelago, the magical evening light, getting up early to go fishing, the sound of waves crashing against the rocks. The sea always gave me a sense of freedom. This became clearer for me as my career advanced, when I hardly saw anything but hotel rooms and airport terminals.

Resarö was also the place where my parents first met. Though they were so young when they fell in love, they got married and stayed together for their whole lives. They came from two different parts of the small island, Överby on the one side and

Ytterby on the other, and met at the dance floor in the middle. Throughout my life I've often admired their ability to stick together, both when things were going well and when things were tough.

My parents had their own boat in Södertälje, an old Pettersson boat that they'd inherited from my grandfather, and we could take it all the way to Resarö. It was always a wonderful journey, I would just lie in the cabin and eat candy. We would always pass through Stockholm and the whole archipelago, and would usually come ashore in the village of Sandhamn on the island of Sandö so I could play a bit of tennis. I'm sure it was in everyone's interest that I got a chance to run around and burn off all the energy I had in me. Once we arrived in Resarö, it was all about badminton instead. We'd string up a net between two trees, and then the competitions would begin.

All the adults in the family thought I was completely mad, totally off my rocker. If I lost, I went completely nuts. I'd have to go lie down in a little house in the yard, even if it was the middle of the afternoon. Mum would say, 'You're not coming out until you've pulled yourself together. Are you going to behave now? Have you learned anything?'

But I always came out just as angry – and had to go back in again. It was the same whenever we played Monopoly or other games.

Though the summers were idyllic, it never took long before I was yearning for home in Södertälje. This was because I looked forward to indoor training. But when I was twelve years old, something happened that upended everything for a while: I was suspended for bad behaviour. The punishment was completely fair – I had misbehaved on the court, cheated, thrown the racket and embarrassed myself.

The next day, the club management called my parents and told them what had happened. My parents were probably even more ashamed than I was. The management said I'd be severely punished, that this behaviour could absolutely not be tolerated. At the same time, they were quite kind to me because they chose to delay the punishment until the winter season when I was playing ice hockey instead. But I had learnt a lesson. I was never going to lose my temper on a tennis court again, and I was never going to embarrass myself like that in front of my parents.

It was probably at that moment that I decided not to show any emotion during a match either. I think it was something that served me well throughout my career, it gave me a special kind of strength in difficult situations, a psychological advantage. My nickname later became 'Ice-Borg', and most people probably thought that it came about organically, as if it simply reflected how I've always been as a person. I don't think anyone realised that it was the result of the bitter experiences of a twelve-year-old.

Life is made up of coincidences. One lucky one for me was that one of the world's best tennis coaches at the time, Percy Rosberg, one day happened to be in Södertälje. What characterised Percy was that he was a master at refining the technique of his trainees. Many of us tennis players in Sweden owe him a lot. After working with me, he also came to train future generations of the Swedish 'tennis wonder', including players like Stefan Edberg and Magnus Norman.

Percy was in Södertälje to watch junior tennis and to scout for interesting new talents. Many people wanted to attend the lesson he was going to give for the younger players, but I wasn't eligible because I was too young. But as it happened, someone fell ill at the last minute, and they figured I could step in and take the spot. Percy took an instant liking to the way I played. He told my parents that he saw a real winner and a talent that he wanted to help develop. I couldn't believe it, since all the other players that were chosen were at least four years older than me! But there was a catch. In order to train with Percy, you had to go to SALK – Stockholms Allmänna Lawntennis Klubb – which was located in Bromma, and to attend required my parents' approval as well as a lot of sacrifices.

Bromma is almost four miles from Södertälje. For me, the distance was not only geographical, just saying the name felt like a big deal to a little Södertälje boy like me. In addition, I would get to play and train with guys who were several years older than me and whom I looked up to. Would they be nice to me or treat me like the country kid? I had no idea, but I knew I'd do anything to train with Percy and to do it at SALK. The geographical problem was solved by being able to take the commuter train back and forth. My parents were unable to drive me, but on Wednesdays my grandfather would come and pick me up. I spent many hours on those commuter trains, which often had to stop whenever there were too many leaves piled up on the tracks or if there had been too much snow in the winter. I spent many hours on cold station platforms, waiting for trains that never seemed to arrive.

But there I was, every day, with my training bag, longing for nothing else other than to keep training and playing tennis. I can still see that little guy in front of me today, that boy who is still within me, how his dedication made all the problems and obstacles fade away as if they meant nothing.

My grades suffered, of course. All the time I spent travelling made school feel like a necessary evil. Except for when I had to do my workplace internship in year 8, when I was 14 or so. Then I was able to combine training at SALK with my internship at the evening newspaper *Aftonbladet*'s sports editorial office, which was located in the Klara neighbourhood in central Stockholm. One day I might accompany a journalist on an assignment to interview some sports person. It was fantastic for a teenager like me to do an internship there, because sport was all I thought about. During the second week of my internship, I got to hang out with a sports teacher in Södertälje. So it was sport through and through and it couldn't have been a coincidence. The staff at the school must have helped out to make sure I got such good internships.

At some point during secondary school, the Swedish Tennis Association also started to get involved. They saw potential in me and wanted to give me the chance to play even more. I know that people from the association had gone to my school to persuade the head teacher to let me go to a training camp early in the season. I was thrilled when the school decided to cut me some slack when it came to my attendance, giving me an opportunity to fully commit to tennis.

Towards the end of secondary school, it became really difficult to keep up with classes because tennis was now taking up all my waking hours. I was playing more and more and travelling farther and farther away, sometimes abroad. In 1972, when I was still in year 9, I was even selected in Sweden's team for the Davis Cup. It was a huge deal. The tournament, a team competition between countries, was legendary and had been going on since the beginning of the century.

To keep up with everything, the school arranged for me to finish the term early, after I had taken the exams in my main subjects of Swedish, German and English. After all, it was compulsory education, and I needed to get final grades in those subjects. Luckily, I had understanding teachers who helped me with this arrangement.

Travelling to other countries is also a kind of education, so it was almost comical when I had to sit and answer simple questions from my teacher in English. I was already quite used to other languages.

But the school administrators at Blombacka really stood up for me, there's nothing else I can say. Apparently, it was the first time a situation like this had arisen at a Swedish school, so they had no protocols to deal with it. But they handled it well and today there are even some sports schools meant for those who want to pursue a career in sport.

Whenever I travelled, I always used to send postcards from the places I visited to friends, family and of course to my mum and dad. The postcards were quite wordy, but I thought it was fun, and it was a way for me to keep in touch with them back home, even when I was far away. That was as close as we came to social media in those days. Not long ago I was reminded of those postcards when I met an old school friend from Södertälje and she showed me all the cards I had sent her. It was truly touching to learn that she had saved them for all those years.

It was Percy Rosberg who helped me to improve my technique, some of which I had invented on my own, such as the two-handed forehand and the two-handed backhand. Percy thought it looked crazy at first and tried to talk me out of it, but he soon realised that I was stubborn on that point and he gave up. With his help, I eventually switched to hitting forehand with one hand. Percy was criticised a lot by other coaches for his two-handed backhand, but he shook it off and helped me refine the technique. For example, there were certain situations where I obviously benefited from dropping the two-hand, such as volleys up at the net.

The training paid off. I won more junior championships and

my match results steadily improved. A couple of times I also won the school championship that took place in Bromma in the winter. The tournament still exists today and is one of the largest junior competitions in Sweden. The summer of 1970 was the first year of the Kalle Anke Cup tournament played in Båstad, and I won my category, boys born 1955–6. A girl of the same age called Helena Anliot won her category. She won not only this competition, but also my heart.

Helena became the first great love of my youth and, since we both played tennis, we were able to see each other from time to time. We were together for several years but we weren't always able to spend much time together, with our respective playing schedules. Many people thought Helena would go far as a tennis player, something she certainly had the talent to accomplish. She went on to win the Australian Hardcourt Championship, the Swedish Open in Båstad and other major titles. Later in life, she told me how much she had disliked the attention that came with my breakthrough, that so much was written about us being a couple. We were hounded by photographers and journalists and her own life as a tennis player was increasingly overshadowed. She has written a very powerful book about her reasons for ending her promising tennis career so early.

It's pretty amazing that there were so many competitions for us young tennis players. In addition to the Swedish School Championships, the Junior Championships and the Kalle Anke Cup, there was also another important tournament: Kungens Kanna, the King's Pitcher. It was played in the Royal Tennis Hall and it was none other than the King himself who presented the prize. What characterised Kungens Kanna at the time was that it was a tournament with handicap rules based on the players' rankings. If you were playing against a better player, the scoring would be to your advantage, and if you were playing against someone who was lower ranked than yourself it was the other way round.

In 1970, I was fourteen and made it to the final, where I lost to Magnus Feldt, who was seven years older. But what changed my life in that tournament was that a certain Lennart 'Labbe' Bergelin caught my eye. After the match, he came up to me on the centre court and said that I had played very well.

'What an idiot!' I thought.

3

Labbe Steps In

I have to admit that I didn't know who Labbe was when he came up to introduce himself, that tall man who thought I had played well despite losing the match. Someone explained to me that he worked for the Swedish Tennis Association and that he was one of Sweden's most distinguished tennis players ever. That of course made me more interested.

In the 1940s and '50s Labbe had been ranked among the world's best players and his main weapons were his serve and his strong forehand. Another strength was his incredible ability to concentrate, something he saw as a prerequisite for success in tennis. He was the first Swede to win a Grand Slam when he and Jaroslav Drobný won the French Open doubles in 1948, but he is probably best remembered for playing in a remarkable Davis Cup match against Australia in 1950 when he defeated the great Frank Sedgman. The match was played on grass, and it had rained so much that Labbe eventually chose to play the fifth and decisive set barefoot! He was actually awarded the daily newspaper *Svenska Dagbladet*'s medal of honour after winning the match.

When I first met Labbe, he was working for the Tennis Association. He had at his disposal a grey Volkswagen bus that he used to shuttle around young people eager to compete, he could take with him two girls and five boys. He offered me a spot in the bus and that's when it all really got started, when my tennis world expanded. We went from playing everywhere in Sweden to suddenly competing in the other Nordic countries and Europe.

The atmosphere in the bus was incredible when we were out on the road. Labbe's huge heart was dedicated to tennis and he was fantastic with us juniors. At the same time, he could have a short temper and you had to watch out when you were teasing him that you didn't set him off. One time when we juniors were playing in Monte Carlo, Labbe was also playing in a senior competition there. We were sitting in the stands cheering him on when someone came up with the idea that we should have a bit of fun with him. Labbe had a clear lead in the match and we asked an official we knew to tell him that he had received an important phone call. Labbe got very worried when the official signalled: 'Come up and take a call'.

Since he was playing on the centre court, there were steep stairs up to the secretary's office and Labbe ran faster than I had ever seen him run before. Of course, when he got there, there was no one on the phone. He was furious, and it didn't get any better when he realised that we kids were the culprits. Thankfully he won the match anyway and I think he won the whole tournament too. Not many people were able to beat him at that time. Despite the comfortable win, we juniors had to keep our distance for a while. As I said, Labbe had both a big heart and a fiery temper.

To my great joy, I was now part of Labbe's team of young players. In the legendary bus, three of us sat at the back, three in the middle and one in the front seat next to Labbe. For a bunch of restless youngsters like us, it was a challenge to sit still for so many hours. In the bus you sometimes had to take a nap, but often there was a lot of cackling and everyone was talking at each other. There was no radio, so we had a portable tape recorder with us to listen to music. There was a lot of Elvis Presley at a constantly high volume.

Sometimes we had to travel really long distances in the bus, such as when we went to Denmark, Germany, England, France and Spain. We never slept in the bus, trying instead to find the cheapest motels along the way. On one memorable occasion, the bus broke down and we were left on the side of the road. It didn't take long before someone stopped to help, because we probably looked both lost and innocent standing there outside the bus. I was all thumbs when it came to mechanical things, but Labbe was not at all unskilled when it came to fixing broken cars, as long as he had the right tools. I saw him walk over to the stopped car. The driver rolled down the window and I heard him ask if they could help with anything. Then I heard Labbe's characteristic Swenglish: 'Do you have what we in Sweden call a *skiftnyckel*?' God knows how they managed to figure out what he needed was an adjustable spanner.

One time, when we were playing in London, our bus ended up at Piccadilly Circus. Labbe hated driving on the left side of the road, and the English roundabouts were the worst of all because in his head they went the wrong way. We went round and round for several minutes just because he couldn't find the right exit. The louder we laughed, the more frustrated Labbe became among the honking cars and double-decker buses pushing their way through. I can't imagine how he put up with us at such moments, I would have just parked the bus and walked away. In retrospect, I'm impressed by Labbe's stubbornness and commitment.

Even then, Labbe had his own unique way with metaphors, which would eventually make him popular far beyond tennis circles. My personal favourites are: 'A good laugh extends the jaw' and 'You mustn't be stupid or you'll end up the head coach.'

My own nickname 'Burken' – 'The Jar' – also came about during this time and it's no secret that it was Labbe who coined it. He thought it suited me perfectly, I was a jar with the lid on, everything remained locked up in there. Labbe meant no offence and he didn't say it in a derogatory way, but it was clear that he meant something by it. I myself have never minded my nickname, even after I became famous and others started using it. A lot of my old tennis mates still call me Burken and I've never taken offence.

One of the first tournaments Labbe took us to was in Berlin. Unlike in Sweden, Europe didn't have a system of age categories, so the guys I played against were usually two or three years older than me. Though I was so young, the others on the team respected and encouraged me. The matches went my way, I won my category and the journey continued to Mönchengladbach. Much to my and Labbe's delight, I won there too and it was after that victory that people started talking about me in tennis circles: 'Who's that little blond guy from Sweden who has a style all his own?'

Pretty soon Labbe and others at the Tennis Association realised that more money was needed to keep the momentum going. My family didn't have the resources themselves but fortunately the affluent Swedish family Wallenberg stepped in and created a fund to help finance my trips. As the victories increased, so

I was offered sponsorship deals for rackets, clothing and other equipment. My first contract for clothes and shoes was with Fred Perry. I didn't really care much about my appearance, but from the outside, the venture looked undeniably professional. Dad helped me negotiate a good deal with Templeman, the company that represented Slazenger in Sweden, so that I got ten thousand kronor a year.

Suddenly I found myself in a world of opportunity. I was a sulky fourteen-year-old, in the throes of puberty, who hated to lose but loved to win. Now I was good enough to take part in the Swedish Open for real and in 1972 it was held indoors in Umeå. I reached the semi-finals but lost in five sets. In my day, the vast majority of matches were played over the best of five sets – today, that only happens in the big Grand Slam tournaments.

In August the following year, the Swedish Open was held outdoors, in Västerås. I had turned sixteen and in the final I met Ove Bengtson, who together with Jan-Erik Lundqvist had dominated Swedish men's tennis since the 1960s. Ove had won the Swedish Championship four times and certainly looked impressive with his beard and his two metres of height. He also had a good first serve and was often on the attack right out of the gate.

I won three sets in a row to become the youngest Swedish tennis champion of all time. Perhaps it was something of a breakthrough for me, at least in Sweden. Imagine that later in the '70s Ove and I would play many doubles matches together in the Davis Cup. In addition, he and his wife Lotta helped me a lot and the three of us would often travel together, almost like a family, for all sorts of tennis engagements. So it was absolutely correct when Ove described himself as a big brother and mentor to me.

*

1972 is the year when my international career really took off. I focused on playing as many junior competitions as I could abroad and with the constant travelling, I was hardly ever at home. Even then, my family and others around me realised that my teenage years would not be like others'. I didn't have many friends of the same age to socialise with, there was no partying and no concerts. So it was comforting when, much later, my mum reminded me of one of the annual holiday parties from that time.

Someone had rung the doorbell, but when she opened it no one was there. After a while she saw me, lying on a sled. I was obviously quite drunk, and I myself have no recollection of what might have happened that night. I probably didn't then either but I likely had a splitting headache the next day. I had apparently been having fun with some neighbourhood friends, perhaps a little too much fun. But it was kind of them to pull me home in a sled before thanking me for a nice evening.

Whenever I was home and could be a 'normal' teenager, it was a liberating exception to the daily routine of my then sixteen-year-old life. Many people thought I was living a glamorous life with all the travelling around the world. That wasn't quite true. When we played abroad, for example in Costa Rica, which organised the Coffee Bowl, or in the Dominican Republic, we often stayed with host families.

My son Leo actually met my old host family in Costa Rica when he played there a few years ago. He went to visit the family and it turned out that they had saved the sheets I had slept in fifty years earlier. Apparently they had a feeling that I was going to be something big. Leo and I laughed out loud at the story and at the same time were deeply touched by their incredible hospitality. They were good at showing off Costa Rica to all of us who travelled there. We juniors were to see as much of the country as possible, including going horse riding. I've always been a bit scared of horses, but at least I got on the back of a horse – only to fall off again just as quickly. This is where I got my first serious injury, a big fracture in my wrist, but luckily it was the left one. I had to put a cast on my hand and forfeit the match in the tournament I was playing in.

The Orange Bowl in Florida was the highest ranked junior championship, above even Wimbledon. I won the competition in 1971 in the boys' under-16 category and the following year, 1972, I won the under-18 category when I beat Vitas Gerulaitis in three straight sets. That was the first time our paths crossed.

At junior Wimbledon in 1971, I was knocked out in the first round, but the following year I was ready for revenge. I made it all the way to the final and was up against the Briton Buster Mottram, who was a year older and the son of two famous British tennis players. He had a good serve and was happy to go to the net, whereas I had refined my baseline game. Buster himself has said that he was quite confident before the match, thinking that my game wouldn't suit the Wimbledon grass as well as his faster volleying. That was probably the general opinion of everyone who had seen me play. Nevertheless, I made it all the way to the final.

My strongest memory from that day is not the match itself, which I managed to win after being down 5–2 in the final set. Nor that I got to lift the winners' trophy for the first time. No, my strongest memory was that before the match I had the opportunity to warm up with the extremely charismatic Romanian Ilie Năstase, who on the same day would play the Wimbledon final against the gentlemanly American Stan Smith, ranked number one in the world. Ilie was ranked third and as well as being one of the fastest players – he could save impossible balls – he was also entertaining. The crowd loved him when he put on a show and made faces and did funny gestures.

As soon as my match was over and I had won, I took a quick shower and hurried to Centre Court to watch the men's final. Luckily, the match was a long one and I had just made it to the first game of the fifth set. It was my first time on Centre Court and the first time I had ever seen such a big and important match in person. I couldn't even imagine that four years later I would be standing in the same place and actually beating Năstase, even if I always dreamed big.

I watched as the tall, handsome Stan Smith fought and kept his composure against the more wild, outgoing Năstase. The stands were silent and the tension was thick in the air. The match had swung back and forth and was now completely even, but in the end it was Smith who won 7–5 in the fifth set.

I was ecstatic. This final had everything anyone could want a tennis match to be. The silence between balls, the laconic voice of the umpire announcing the score, the clouds heavy with rain, the roar of the crowd when a player made a simple mistake, the cheers when a ball was settled by a perfect shot – the whole arena was like a boiling cauldron.

Of course, I was rooting for Ilie a little more after the incredible experience of warming up with him a few hours earlier, but I had to admit that Stan Smith's calmness had won the match fair and square. His coolness impressed me. At the same time, as soon as he won the match, it was as if his whole body erupted in a single victory roar. He became like a different person, showing emotion and wild joy, jumping over the net and hugging Năstase, who somewhat resignedly thanked the crowd by lifting his racket in greeting.

There I was, the little guy from Södertälje, witnessing a great match, something I had previously only dreamed of. Now I was one step closer to the big league.

4

The World Becomes
My Arena

When Sweden played Australia in the Davis Cup final in Båstad in 1964, tennis fever was taking over the country. At the time Australia was the great power in tennis, and Dad and I were sitting in front of the black-and-white screen in the living room, as was the rest of Sweden. The sport of tennis had slowly but surely grown in popularity throughout the country and now we were intensely involved in the match. We cheered for Ulf Schmidt and Jan-Erik Lundqvist against Roy Emerson and Fred Stolle. The favourites Australia kept up the pressure and won the matches easily, 5–0. Despite the loss, the games were defining moments for me. I was impressed by how well they played. I was only eight years old when I saw it on TV, but even then there was something magical about tennis.

Interest in tennis increased in Sweden after that sensational match against Australia in the Davis Cup final. But then came a few years without success, and the Swedish Tennis Association wanted to see a revival. It was around that time that the national coach, Labbe, took an interest in me and saw an opportunity to bring in someone new and unexpected. He and the others at the Association knew that I was promising, but at the same time I was so young and therefore a wild card.

Everyone took it for granted that Ove Bengtson and Jan-Erik Lundqvist would be selected to represent Sweden in the 1972 Davis Cup, because they were the two most experienced singles players. But before the Davis Cup, there was a large group going to Madrid for a tournament and, as usual, Labbe drove us down in his Volkswagen bus. By chance I got to meet Jan-Erik in the tournament and somewhat unexpectedly I won that match. This in turn led to me being offered a place in the Davis Cup team.

To play the Davis Cup in Båstad at the age of fifteen was an incredibly huge deal. On 5 May 1972, in my first match, we faced New Zealand. I was to play against Onny Parun, who the year before had reached the quarter-finals at Wimbledon and was among the twenty best in the world. Pretty soon it looked bleak because I was two sets down and 3–0 down in the third.

What happened next were only small things, but things that decided the match in an unexpected way. Maybe my opponent started to think that the match was already won, maybe he just lost his rhythm. In any case, at this point Parun protested a referee's decision, blaming it on a ball boy. It wasn't a big deal, but the umpire forced him to replay his serve.

During the whole exchange, I just stood there without showing any emotion at all. More than anything else I probably just looked bored. But the fact is that I was still in the middle of the match, preparing for the next ball. I hadn't given up. I knew that if I won this game and went 3–1, I could serve out the next one. Then I just had to break his serve one more time and the third set would be even. In other words, the set was still winnable. And after that I could win the next two sets and the whole match. I knew the way to get there was to win point by point.

That's exactly what happened. I won six straight games in the third set, and then won the next two sets 6–4, 6–4. The crowd around the centre court in Båstad was elated and applauded like crazy. It shouldn't have been possible for an unknown fifteen-year-old to beat a world-class player, especially after being so far behind.

The strange thing is that I remember very little of the match itself, even though it should've been the greatest thing I had ever experienced as a tennis player. But I do remember that I was proud that Labbe was praised – because he had had the courage to put me on the team.

It was only afterwards that I learnt that I was the youngest player ever to win a Davis Cup match. Since then, there's been a plethora of young players, both boys and girls, who have won and who were younger than I was. It got to the point where they had to impose an age limit of fourteen to play in the Davis Cup at all. After the breakthrough against New Zealand, I lost three singles matches in the Davis Cup, but between 1973 and 1980 I didn't lose a single one. I managed thirty-three straight wins in the tournament.

Although I've always considered myself a very individual athlete, this type of team match seemed to suit me perfectly. You play singles matches, but you win and lose as a team. Unfortunately, that year we were eliminated in the next match when we lost 3–1 to Czechoslovakia in Prague.

Having won junior Wimbledon in 1972, I now had a wildcard into the senior US Open, to be played on grass at Forest Hills. For talented younger players, getting a wildcard is significant because it allowed us to play at a higher level without having to meet the usual entry requirements. In the first round, I faced Roy Emerson and lost three sets to one. I wasn't ready for these events yet, but at the same time I needed to gain experience to one day make it to the seniors.

One particular thing characterised that match against Emerson more than anything else, a funny encounter that I can still laugh about when I think about it. During the match I felt annoyed and frustrated, because I couldn't get my game to flow at all. It didn't help that one of the ball boys was completely useless and couldn't throw the ball to me properly. How hard could it be? Later on I found out that that annoying ball boy was none other than John McEnroe.

The following year, 1973, things started to spin even faster because now I had more experience and was ready to take on the big boys. It started with me getting the chance to play in the French Open in Paris. The tournament started off pretty well, I won the first three matches, but then I went out in the round of 16 against the Italian Adriano Panatta. A few days after the loss, I celebrated my seventeenth birthday. I still had a lot to learn.

Then it was time to turn my attention to Wimbledon. I wasn't actually ranked high enough to play that year, but because of a player boycott, many people skipped the tournament. The row had originated in a dispute over whether or not Yugoslavian player Nikola Pilić should be forced to represent his country in the Davis Cup. Over eighty players boycotted the tournament, but I, being so young, hadn't yet joined a players' association, so I was completely out of the conflict and there was nothing to prevent my participation. Perhaps it was also because of the boycott that Premjit Lall and I got to play on Centre Court as soon as the first round.

In any case, I made it to the quarter-finals where I faced the local talent Roger Taylor, thirty-one years old, left-handed and difficult to play. After a bad start for me, the match evened out and went to a fifth and final set. Unfortunately, I lost my rhythm, my game was not right and I was defeated. Maybe it was again due to my lack of experience, but I felt strongly that I should've won the match. So mentally I wasn't that far behind any more.

As I started winning more matches and rising higher and higher in the rankings, I was now playing in all the important tournaments. This also meant that I was being recognised on a completely different level. People started talking about me as a teenage idol, some even called me a 'rock star'. This was also after the hysteria of Beatlemania. At first I didn't realise what they were doing. Of course, I'd been noticing more girls following my matches, hearing them shouting out for me, but now it was taking on whole new proportions. Sometimes the organisers had to install guards to discourage girls from running onto the court at the first opportunity and disrupting the match. You don't see that any more, now everything's organised in a completely different way.

People have asked me how it felt, when girls would shout and scream at me. It was flattering for a young guy, of course, but it was also a bit annoying because it interfered with my preparation and made it harder for me to perform as well as I wanted. If I had been given the choice, I would've escaped from it, but it was already something that I didn't like to even think about. They only wanted me to do my best, they were cheering me on, why should I be ungrateful and complain? Even my opponents were bothered, but mostly we players laughed about it, it was like some kind of hysteria that brought new crowds to tennis. And it was also no secret that I was quite fond of girls, but at the same time much shyer than everyone thought.

This wasn't just about me, because during these years something bigger was happening to tennis. It went from being a classic sport, with a small number of players and spectators, to becoming incredibly popular, with us tennis players transforming into heroes and teen idols. For this to be possible, we players had to develop our own personalities and playing styles, which is how the fans were able to have their personal favourites. Of course, the sport itself was bigger than us individual players, but many people still thought there was something special about us. I think I stood out because I was so young, a bit quiet and enigmatic.

In those early years, I did my best to manage my poor English and my Swedish accent. Journalists were happy to make fun of me, especially in England, and sometimes it was terribly irritating. You have to remember that I was very young, plus I never liked talking. It wasn't my thing then, and it's not my thing now. I do it because I have to, though it's easier today because I have more control over the contexts in which I'm expected to say something. It's easier now to reflect on what happened, it was much harder when I was in the middle of it. Today, young players receive a completely different media training than in my time, when you were basically thrown to the wolves and had to do your best to figure it out.

Arthur Ashe was one of the really big players on the tour when I broke through. As well as being a fantastic tennis player, he also meant a great deal to the sport of tennis in general. For a long time, tennis was called the 'white sport'. I myself came from relatively ordinary surroundings in Södertälje and received great support from both the Tennis Association and special youth initiatives that were often non-profit, but tennis was considered to be something that mainly the upper classes played.

What Arthur Ashe stood for was to show how the sport was something much more.

Today, tennis is a global sport with players coming from all parts of the world, and it's also gratifying to see how women's tennis today has as high a status as men's tennis. To reach that point, it took pioneers like Ashe. In addition to being an important spokesperson for tennis, he also showed great courage when, in 1992, he openly told people that he had contracted AIDS after a blood transfusion, at a time when almost no one talked about the disease or dared to make public the fact that they had become ill. The terrible disease took his life just a year later and it seems only right that the centre court of the venue that currently hosts the US Open bears his name: the Arthur Ashe Stadium.

Many people in the US have told me that the first time they heard of me was when I faced Arthur Ashe in the third round of the 1973 US Open. He was seeded third and a huge home favourite, there was a heatwave in New York and the crowd was as loud as ever. By then, I had caught the eye of some on the other side of the Atlantic, as I was something of a star and had made it to the quarter-finals of Wimbledon – and not just because of the boycott. People now knew that I could play well even on grass.

When the draw came out, a lot of people wanted to see me play Ashe, hoping for an exciting encounter between the favourite and the up-and-comer in the third round. The media pressure was enormous, suddenly everyone wanted to see me and Arthur play.

And so it was.

In the US Open the players didn't have to play in all-white outfits like in other tournaments. Ashe played in an unbuttoned tight red and white check shirt, with a big wooden necklace. He had a cool haircut and big sideburns. I wore a turquoise shirt and yellow-and-blue sweatbands around my wrists. I wasn't very nervous – he was the one who had all the pressure on him, whereas I could relax and simply play good tennis.

Ashe had won the first set after a tiebreak and I the next two. The decisive moment came in the fourth set. I managed to break his serve and now the question was whether my nerve would hold for the next two service games, so that I could win the match. They held – and in fact I played really well the whole match, from the first ball to the last. It was by far my biggest win of the year and the best grass court match of my career so far.

Everyone was surprised that I beat Ashe, both the journalists and the crowd. This was still 1973 and I had now proved to myself and others that I could beat the big names, fight at the top of the world. The win paved the way for me into 1974 and playing the Italian Open in Rome and the French Open in Paris. And with it came the self-confidence – I had no fear of these players any more. The match against Arthur Ashe was my big breakthrough in the USA, although I lost in the next round against the left-handed veteran Nikola Pilić from Yugoslavia and had to exit the tournament.

Nor did I show any great skill in dealing with journalists. I ended up saying some weird things like how I liked playing in New York more than Wimbledon because 'the girls left me alone here'.

On the way home from the US Open, something unexpected happened. When I got to the airport in New York, Helena suddenly turned up. It had been a while since we had seen each other, and now she was also on her way home after playing a tournament in the US. Neither of us had any idea that the other would be there.

That's how rarely we saw each other and how difficult it was to keep in touch in those days, it was long before the age of mobile phones and other ways of being in constant contact. But when we did meet, it was as if no time had passed, everything was the same and we liked each other a lot. It was such a happy accident that we ran into each other at the airport; both of us were equally delighted and surprised when we saw each other. On the flight home, our love began to bloom and when we stopped over in Copenhagen, we decided to stay there for a couple of days, just enjoying each other and time together.

When we parted ways, we knew it would be a long while before we saw each other again.

5

The Climb to the Top

I had risen rapidly in the world rankings and after the 1973 US Open I was ranked number eighteen. That autumn it was once again time for my home tournament – the Stockholm Open at the Royal Tennis Hall. This year it felt different to be there, because my self-confidence had grown so much. I still had to fight my way through round by round, but I managed to both knock out the world number one, Ilie Năstase, and get revenge on Nikola Pilić in tough matches. The big match for me in this tournament would be the semi-final, where I was to face Jimmy Connors for the first time.

Jimmy 'Jimbo' Connors is one of the tennis players I've gone up against the most in my career. We've played over twenty matches – and often very decisive ones like quarters, semis or finals. The first few times it was usually Jimmy who won, but later in my career it was the other way round. To put it simply, he beat me at the US Open and I beat him at Wimbledon.

When we faced each other for the first time, I was seventeen years old and Jimmy had turned twenty-one. He had already won sixteen titles and gone far in several Grand Slam tournaments. I knew he had a special technique, that he took the ball early and returned it hard and with a flat hit rather than with a lot of topspin, a technique that came to inspire many of the players who came after us. While I had had to fight my way through to the semi-finals, Jimmy had won all his matches easily. But if he went in as the favourite on paper, I had stronger crowd support. The Royal Tennis Hall holds up to four thousand spectators and nearly every one of them was loudly cheering for me.

All three sets ended up even, but in the last one it came right down to the wire. We held our serve and went into a decisive tiebreak. Once I was there, I quickly gained the upper hand and was able to close out the match. The crowd cheers went through the roof and you could tell Jimmy thought he'd played as much against everyone in the stands. He would get his revenge on that front when we later played in New York, when the crowd was huge and on his side.

After this exciting match, the tournament ended with a narrow loss in the final to another American, Tom Gorman. I'm not usually one to complain about referees, but I knew a key shot of mine had been wrongly called out in the tiebreak in the final set. It's not an excuse, but when you've played so much tennis, you can actually feel if a ball is in.

At the time, there was no electronic Hawk-Eye to see if the ball was in or not. Some of the charm of the sport was probably lost when the judgements were automated, but you then didn't have the frustration that comes from the limitations of the human eye. Regardless of what happened in that particular match, there is no tennis player who hasn't experienced this situation. When you summarise your career, it probably comes down to one thing – all the times bad calls went your way and all the times they went your opponent's way.

I had to chew on the final loss, but it was also important to remind myself of the matches I had won, several of them in evenly matched tiebreakers. I already knew that I was on my game for the most important balls, and now my opponents knew it too. Being able to handle the pressure is an important quality for a tennis player, because it's not about who wins the most balls. You have to win the *right* ones.

The climb to the top of the world continued steadily and in November I was in the top ten. In November I went to Buenos Aires for the ATP tournament, the only worldwide tour for the best men's players, organised by the Association for Tennis Professionals. I made it to the final, which was played in front of packed stands with home idol Guillermo Vilas on the other side of the net. He was the king of Argentina and of course everyone was rooting for him. I was 2–1 up and the stands were dead silent, except for one ice-cream vendor who kept shouting: 'Helado! Helado!' I finally lost my temper with him and went up to the referee and tried to make myself understood, even though both of us were speaking broken English.

'Can you shut this guy up?' I asked.

Everyone in the stands thought this was the most entertaining thing they'd seen in a long time, they enjoyed watching my mounting frustration. I should've kept my cool, but instead I became even more agitated.

Maybe it was karma kicking in. In the tiebreak of the fourth set, Guillermo got a lob over me. I tried to run backwards but fell over the linesman's chair and hurt my back so badly that I had to stop the match. It was one of the more annoying losses of my career, tripping over a chair. I was so disappointed to finish in such a way, especially since I had been well placed to win the match.

South America had more surprises in store. After the disappointing exit, I joined some other players in Rio de Janeiro. A couple of days later we were all going back to Europe for further matches, and we thought we could use a couple of days off, just to hang around the area and be able to relax. We were staying near the famous beach at Copacabana and decided to go for a swim. The sun was shining and the sea beckoned. I'm quite a good swimmer and if I'm going to jump in ideally the water should be at least twenty-five degrees. Swimming is something I can do. If you grew up in the archipelago it was a natural part of summer activities.

I'm not sure what happened this time, if the water was too rough or if it was the waves that took me, but I was taken further and further out from the shore. It was too late when I realised what was happening – that I was in real danger and that I had to try to get inland. But it was impossible, there was no way I could manage to swim back. I tried to stay calm, one stroke after the other, but the current only pulled me further out. It was useless. I felt my strength fading and panic washing over me.

I remember raising a hand in the air to see if anyone would see me and come to my aid, but I had drifted too far out and the other swimmers were far away. Luckily someone spotted my flailing arms and there was a flurry of activity. Several guys with surfboards came paddling out towards me. When they finally dragged me to the shore I was coughing and throwing up water, but I managed to get my breath and come out of the darkness.

The real shock came a few days later, when I realised how close it had been. I could well have drowned, but I survived by the skin of my teeth and a few days later I went home to Sweden.

In fact, that's not the only time I've come close to drowning.

It happened again, many years later, when I was with some friends in Cannes on the French Riviera. We had hired a boat and travelled down to Corsica and Sardinia. Between the two islands we dropped anchor and went for a swim. We knew the water was rough in the strait, we had been warned, but the same thing happened this time, even faster than I could have imagined. I swam for my life but only drifted further away from the boat. I remembered the experience and panic from Rio de Janeiro. 'This isn't happening,' I thought, 'not again.'

And I was paralysed by the memory of Rio, the resignation at the fact that I had once again been swept away by the current with no way to swim back. Thankfully, a friend saw that I was in trouble and dived in to save me. In my panic, I pulled him under too, but by this time the alarm had gone off and the captain threw out a lifebuoy and we were both pulled towards the boat.

I could've died that time too. And I could've dragged my friend down with me into the dark, I was so scared and confused. I had to learn to respect the forces of nature and that life is fragile.

6

The Triumph in Paris

My best years were between 1974 and 1981, eight intense years which laid the foundations for my whole life as a tennis player and a human being. Fundamentally I was the same person, but life in those years gave me so many experiences, for better or worse.

In the beginning I had a lot of help from Mats Hasselquist and Thomas Hallberg from the Swedish Tennis Association who travelled with me in support. It was nice to have someone with me, both for companionship and so that I could vent about my matches with them instead of dwelling on bad decisions and failed shots on my own. Mats and Thomas were able to come along thanks to the Swedish Tennis Association paying all their expenses.

But the big difference in 1974 was that Labbe stepped in for real and became my coach, and something of a second dad. Percy Rosberg had been my coach for a long time, but he rarely travelled with me because he had so many other things to keep track of, for example his tennis shop in Båstad. Percy mainly worked with me on technique, how to improve my tennis with small adjustments. Labbe took care of the rest, from training to everything around it. He had played tennis himself and could fully understand what I needed.

I was actually the first player to have my own coach who lived and travelled with me almost all the time. Guillermo Vilas was the next to follow my example, a year later, but I don't think his coach did half of what Labbe did.

Like the daily massages. We both realised that massages were important in enabling you to play match after match. It sounds obvious today, but at the time it was a bit strange to do massage in such a serious way. And one thing should be clear, it was not a gentle massage. Labbe worked his socks off and we were both equally sweaty after a massage session – me because my whole body felt really good, Labbe because he had to work hard for king and country. Many times I tried to get up and say 'Yup, thank you please,' but Labbe just kept going, sometimes for up to two hours. In fact, Labbe continued to give me massages long after my career was over, maybe not daily but still quite often.

Other players eventually heard about Labbe's massage skills and asked if they could also try it out. One time, I think it was in Monte Carlo, Manuel Orantes insisted on a massage from Labbe. He got what he wanted, but the next day he could barely walk, let alone play tennis. He wasn't used to Labbe's rough treatment and withdrew from the tournament.

For me, it was the opposite: if I didn't get a massage from Labbe, my body immediately felt stiff and inflexible. I was convinced that I needed the massages to keep me injury-free through the tough playing and training schedule. Because hard training it certainly was. On a completely different level than my competitors, I am convinced of that. My training was probably more reminiscent of how you train today, very rigorous and holistic. Being in that mode came quite naturally to me, I liked keeping fit and it wasn't something I ever had to force myself to do. My training regime was entirely my own, not even Labbe interfered with that. I think he knew that it was better if I set it up according to my own head. It all came down to my stubbornness and persistence.

In retrospect, it's easy to see how the joy of playing tennis made all the other sacrifices easy. And then came the rewards: I won more and more.

Now the big contracts also started to roll in, with more money involved, but it was still far from what it's like today. We players were always looking for opportunities for extra income, and a few years earlier a gifted man had emerged who knew how to capitalise on it. His name was Lamar Hunt and he was a successful American businessman involved in many sports.

It was Hunt who had helped set up a tour in the 1960s called World Championship Tennis (WCT). There were three qualifying groups of usually ten players each, split into blue, red and green. Points were awarded for each WCT match, and the eight players with the most points qualified for the finals, which took place in Dallas in May each year. It was a new approach to a tennis tournament, including use of tiebreakers and sudden death deuces, and it was also the start of a new era in professional tennis that meant money at whole new levels. Everyone wanted to be in the last eight in the play-offs. And amazingly, I got there.

My qualifying group started playing early in the year, in February 1974. It was the Rothmans International Tennis Tournament at the classic Royal Albert Hall. I sensationally made it to the final, where I beat the Englishman Mark Cox. It was a big deal because all the big names were there and I beat everyone in the group. Later that day I also won the doubles together with Ove Bengtson. It was our first big win together, and I still got two hours of rest between the singles final and the doubles final. In any case, I was now ready for the big final in Dallas. The fact that the prize money in the tournament was a staggering $50,000 didn't lighten the pressure.

This was my first time playing the WCT, and my strongest memories from the three years I participated are of playing against the legendary Rod Laver, who had been my idol since I was a kid. Nicknamed 'The Rocket', he was an Australian gentleman on the court, a fantastic player and the personification of the classic men's game. I faced him seven more times, even though he was at the end of his career.

He was thirty-six years old when we played the final of a 1974 WCT outdoor clay court event in Houston. He won in two straight sets, which was not fun, but worse was that my parents weren't there to see it. They had had to go home that morning to receive the Monday milk delivery to the store. What was my game against Rod Laver compared to a few litres of milk?

After my sensational victories in the WCT, the Italian Championships in Rome were next. I made it to the semi-finals and there I wanted revenge on Guillermo Vilas after the disappointing loss in Buenos Aires. Talk about a psychological challenge – and it wasn't helped by the fact that the match went to the fifth set and had to be stopped because of darkness when the score was 5–5. The tournament organisers decided that the match would be completed the following day and that the winner would face Ilie Năstase, who had already reached the final, later the same day. Hardly an optimal starting point.

However, the next day I won two games quite quickly and

was armed to the teeth when I met Ilie in the final a few hours later. I won in three straight sets. The joy was enormous, but at the same time I immediately turned my attention to the next tournament.

The road to Paris was now open, where I wanted to make a serious attempt to win my first Grand Slam. Many people thought it was too early, that I was still too young. But I had already beaten all the best players on a few occasions, and now I wanted to win the big tournaments too. The French Open started a little slowly, partly because of my sloppy preparation. I had chosen to wait to go to Paris and instead stay at home in Stockholm and train with Percy on Sunday. The idea was that Percy, Labbe and I would travel to Paris the day after – that is, the same day as my first match would be played. Cutting it so close was a rather stupid decision, one might think. Both Labbe and Percy were completely against it.

It was also bound to go wrong right away. I was in trouble in the first round against Jean-François Caujolle, but I got my act together and managed to win in the end, as I did in the next two matches. At that time, the first two rounds were played over the best of three sets, and from the third round it became best of five. There's a big difference between playing three or five sets, because with five sets you have more time to turn a deficit around. So that rule was something that eventually had to be changed. If you were – like me – a patient player, the longer matches suited you. I wore out my opponents.

Sure enough, the next two matches went to five sets. Even in those I was in a bad position, but I managed to turn things round in both – first against the American Erik van Dillen, then against the Mexican Raúl Ramírez. In the semi, I beat the American Harold Solomon in a fluctuating match over four sets.

I was now in the perfect position to achieve the biggest

success of my career so far, winning a grand slam. In my head, I could sometimes get the feeling in situations like this that I could influence the outcome of a match in ways beyond just how I was playing. You might call it superstition or maybe a kind of tic, and during this tournament, a certain French perfume ended up playing a big role. It smelled so good, and I'd worn it for every match. Now it felt crucial to wear it for the final too.

Most experts agreed that I had a chance of beating my final opponent, Manuel Orantes, but he was the strong favourite – especially if you compared our paths to the final. The odds didn't get any better when he easily won the first set, and then the second in a tiebreak. I don't think many people in the stands thought I could turn that deficit around.

But this is what can happen in tennis, it can turn completely around. I may have had a slight advantage because I was never bothered either physically or mentally by the fact that the matches were long. In addition, despite the deficit, I was always convinced that I would win. Early on, I had learnt to focus all my thoughts for an hour, then to do it for two hours, but this year I felt like I could concentrate no matter how long the match took. It was just like when I was training, I only had one thing in my head – the next ball, the next shot. I felt that the pressure was more on Orantes than on me.

What happened next is something I'm often asked about still today: a total turnaround of the match picture. I won the next three sets easily, dropping only two games until match point. My first Grand Slam was a fact. Unfortunately, Percy had gone home after the quarter-finals so he couldn't join the celebrations, but I looked up to the stands and saw an overjoyed Labbe jumping for joy. This was what I had been training for all day, all night and every weekend, in all weathers. I loved tennis and I'd been willing to sacrifice everything to one day win a Grand

Slam final. It's hard to explain what it was like to suddenly stand there and realise that the dream had been accomplished. It was an unreal feeling, but at the same time it had really happened. I had just turned eighteen and was the youngest person ever to win the tournament. Everything I wanted from life had just come true.

In the evening, I went to the Eiffel Tower and had a victory dinner with Labbe and some Swedish journalists. We had almost become mates after all the time we had spent together at tournaments all around the world.

7

The Move to Monte Carlo

Life can change quickly. You can win in Paris one day and the next a letter from the Swedish armed forces arrives in the letterbox at home on Torekällgatan for you. It was a notice that it was time for me to enlist.

Conscription was compulsory in Sweden and you risked punishment if you didn't do your social duty. In his time, Labbe had decided not to enlist, choosing instead to play the Davis Cup in the USA. But as soon as he landed on home ground in Stockholm, he was caught and had to spend some time in jail. It wasn't that bad for me. I turned up for the muster and took all the tests, both physical and psychological, and all the theory.

The results of the physical tests were very good and it was at this point that my low resting heart rate was noticed for the first time, only 32–34 beats per minute. Perhaps this wasn't a surprise, since I had been training hard for several years by this point.

I was posted to Norrland as a paratrooper, which was an

elite unit, but when it was time to move in, I had already been playing tennis all over the world and it felt like a waste of time to do military service, to say the least. After a lot of back and forth, especially between the tennis association and the military authorities, I finally got a discharge. It was a great relief for me.

As soon as I got the news, I was able to go to Wimbledon to try to repeat what I had just achieved in Paris. I arrived at Wimbledon with victories in Rome and Paris under my belt, but I was still considered a dark horse in the tournament. It wasn't surprising because most people saw my game as better suited to clay. Rome and Paris were part of the clay court season, and the grass courts of Wimbledon were something completely different. I had always seen myself as an all-rounder, but at the same time a lot of people seemed to think my game was better suited to the slower clay surface. The serve cannons and volley specialists got more out of the faster, low-bouncing grass. My racket grip was seen as a bit odd, but it allowed me to apply more topspin than most on both backhand and forehand, which was rewarded particularly well on the clay surface. The weakness with the grip was that I had to change when playing in front of the net. And the net game is important when you play on faster surfaces like grass or hard court.

I started Wimbledon with two fairly easy wins, but when I faced the Egyptian veteran Ismail El Shafei in the third round, things came to an abrupt stop. I was playing too defensively and El Shafei was getting good results from his effective serve and volley. I went out in three straight sets. I just had to go home and lick my wounds.

Regardless of successes and setbacks, family was still most important to me. Labbe and others meant a lot, but there was something special about the support I got from Mum and Dad. Not least when things were going badly. They were my biggest supporters and it was nice to be able to come home and sleep in my old boyhood room on Torekällgatan.

My parents worked hard with their shop and tried to get away sometimes when I played, but it was not easy to arrange. As often as I could between tournaments, I also tried to go home to Grandma and Grandpa in Fruängen and play cards with them, which was something that we all three liked. Of course, contact with my old friends had suffered, it was difficult to make it work when you were always travelling. It wasn't helped by the fact that I was constantly being recognised and could never walk down the street unapproached.

This was the year when the perception of me changed radically, especially in the Swedish press. Previously, I had always felt that I had the nation behind me, receiving nothing but support and cheers. There was a kind of national pride in my success on the tennis court, everyone wanted the best for me. For example, I had been awarded the Swedish newspaper *Svenska Dagbladet*'s seventieth medal of honour, one of the surest signs as an athlete that you have become a national hero. It was a fantastic award to receive, not least when you saw which other Swedish sportsmen and women had received it over the years.

In fact, there was nothing to indicate that the fantastic support at home would end. I was as Swedish as one could be and was proud of it. But there was obviously one thing that could upset that – a move to Monaco.

Over the course of the year, my financial situation had changed fundamentally, with prize money pouring in in a way that would have been impossible to imagine just a year earlier. Although I had help from financial advisers, it was clear that

I needed someone with more experience in managing such a specialised situation as being a professional athlete.

The golfer Arnold Palmer and businessman Mark McCormack had started IMG (International Management Group) a few years earlier, an agency that managed sports careers like mine. Mark was convincing in his attempts to persuade me to sign with them. At the same time, I got contracts with Fila for clothing, Diadora for shoes and Donnay for rackets. Mark would be personally involved with me and my tennis career for a long time, which he showed not least by often inviting me and my parents out either in Paris or in London. Then we could sit down in peace and quiet and talk together about the current situation. He had the ability to make us feel that he was doing that little extra for me, that he wanted the best for me.

The first thing Mark realised was that it was very unwise for me to stay in Sweden. Ninety per cent of my income went to tax and he pointed out that although as long as my career lasted, there would be money coming in, at some point it would probably stop. And then there wouldn't be much left of the money I had earned during those successful years. In other words, I needed to review my finances in both the short and long term.

So at the end of the year I moved to Monte Carlo in Monaco. I was one of the first Swedish sports stars to move there, but a couple of years later, a number of other famous Swedes followed my example, like Ingemar Stenmark and most of the Swedish tennis players. And soon sportspeople from other countries began to do the same. But no other Swede was criticised in the same way as I was over it. Politicians and the press said that I was fleeing from taxes. After I won Wimbledon in 1975, one newspaper even wrote that it was a shame I wasn't Swedish – which, of course, I was.

The political climate in Sweden meant that tax policy was

a hot potato. The view of Swedes who were doing well – and making money – was entirely different at the time. The supergroup Abba was another example, and they were also heavily criticised by other Swedes, who thought it was wrong to make a commercial hit and be on the charts. But it was a little different in music. Sports stars had never chosen to move abroad before. When I left Sweden for Monaco, the only Swede living there was Formula 1 star Ronnie Peterson, but he had moved there from London. I went straight from Södertälje to a life in Monte Carlo.

The decision was actually not hard to make, anything else would've been stupid of me. But it had major consequences. The newspaper headlines back home in Sweden accused me of all sorts of things and I was associated with everything that people disliked about tax avoidance and not taking responsibility for the welfare society. I can understand that, but at the same time I think more people can understand me today than they did in the '70s.

Though the Swedish tax system was definitely a major reason for the move, another was to be able to have a base on the continent to reduce the number of long journeys. Sweden was extremely far away from a lot of places. There had been a time when it was possible to take a public bus across Europe, but those days were long gone. Nowadays, flying across the world was the way to go.

It was a big step for me to move from Sweden, because I am Swedish in heart and soul. But one day I had made up my mind. I came home and more or less told my mum and dad that 'now we're moving to Monte Carlo, all three of us.' I needed to keep them close and I didn't want them to miss any more finals because of food deliveries. And so it was that almost on the spur of the moment they decided to sell the shop and move with me.

To this day, I'm impressed by the ease with which they decided to leave everything they knew as home. Even though they
often said they would do anything for me, it was still a big deal
for them to start a new life in a completely unknown country.
They were both in their forties and were now going have to learn
French, a language they had no command of. Even though we
had always been a strong family unit, Mum and Dad were in
danger of being left alone in an environment that must have
seemed like paradise to others.

Surprisingly quickly, however, they made a new life for themselves and enjoyed it. They made themselves more at home in
Monte Carlo than I ever did – I was almost always away playing.
With the move, Mum and Dad decided to find another business. Just a few months later, they opened the Björn Borg Sport
Shop, which meant they kept themselves fully occupied. They
always worked hard, just as they had been taught to do.

In Monte Carlo, a new phase began for all three of us.
Everything was new and big, but somehow didn't feel that way
at all. It was still the three of us. Always.

PART TWO

The Golden Years (1975–1978)

8

The Power of a Pair of Orange Long Johns

Labbe and I never really saw eye to eye on how to plan the year. We often disagreed about which tournaments I should play. I always signed up for more than he thought I should. He thought it was stupid. And looking back, he was almost always right, but I was way too stubborn to admit it at the time.

Having Labbe with me was a huge advantage. He made everything easier and knew exactly what was needed since he'd been a top tennis player himself. He was always honest, sometimes a bit *too* honest, and he always put tennis first. But he also made sure we had fun, which is super important when you're constantly under pressure to play your best.

Tennis is a pretty lonely sport. It's just two players, each on their own side of the net, both doing whatever they can to win, and matches can drag on for more than five hours. Most tournaments are knockout-style, and when you arrive in a new place you never know how long you'll be staying there, if it'll be just one match or six or seven gruelling five-setters in a row.

That loneliness that one could feel while playing tennis is why I liked playing doubles when my schedule allowed it. It was nice to share both the highs and the lows. And I especially loved playing the Davis Cup for Sweden, together with the rest of the team and Labbe as the coach. Sweden had never won the whole thing before, but in 1975 it finally happened.

The Davis Cup really shows how global tennis is. That year, fifty-five teams participated, thirty-two of them from Europe, split into two groups. It began with regional matches earlier in the year, and then the winners from each group met later in the final rounds.

Labbe was the team captain again that year and he symbolised everything that made being on a team so great. Everyone loved joking around with him, and he was a master at keeping the mood light. He was also highly superstitious and had all sorts of strange habits.

One example of that is something that happened during and after the second round against Poland in Warsaw. It was so cold that Labbe wore these absolutely hideous orange long johns with lions on them. They were so appalling it's hard to imagine. But it gets cold when you're the captain and you're stuck sitting on a bench. We ended up winning, and afterwards we all told him that he had to wear those long johns every time we played. That lasted all the way to the semi-finals against the Soviet Union in Latvia's Jūrmala. Even though it was the middle of July and over 30°C , Labbe still sat there wearing his horribly ugly – and horribly warm – long johns. The matches were super close, but we won 3–2. Honestly, Labbe was probably more exhausted than anyone, he nearly sweated to death.

Labbe was a natural entertainer. He had a great singing voice, and at every banquet, he'd always sing the same drinking song: '*Två små röda rosor*' – two small red roses. No party felt complete until he stood up and belted it out with genuine passion. And it was never hard to convince him to, either.

In the European final, we faced the heavily favoured Spain, with strong players like Manuel Orantes and José Higueras. On top of that, they had the home-court advantage in Barcelona. Our team was me, Ove Bengtson, Rolf Norberg and Birger Andersson. Labbe picked me and Birger for the singles, and I played doubles with Ove as usual.

It started off shakily when Birger lost the first singles match against Orantes. I won my singles matches after that, but we'd lost the doubles, so the score was now tied at 2–2. In the final and deciding match, Birger was up against Higueras, who was both higher-ranked and had the home crowd behind him. But things nearly went wrong before the match even started, when Birger realised he'd only brought one racket – the one he was holding in his hand.

Ove had to race back to the hotel to fetch the spare rackets, but he almost couldn't get into his teammate's room because the hotel staff didn't want to let someone else in. Luckily, Ove managed to convince them he was a fellow tennis player and not just some random burglar. The rest of us, still at the arena, could only hope that the lone racket would last long enough for Ove to make it back in time.

Higueras won the first set and had the crowd on his side. But Birger had made incredible comebacks before, and somehow he got inside Higueras' head. He stepped up and absolutely dominated the last two sets, finishing the match 6–0, also known as a 'bagel'. That year, Birger became heroically known as 'Bagel-Birger' across all of Sweden. It was only fair that he got much of the attention. Few matches have ever been as thrilling to watch as when he came back from impossible deficits against higher-ranked players.

Now we were looking ahead to more Davis Cup play at the end of September. Then came the semi-finals at home in Båstad against Chile in September.

While the Davis Cup was underway, I also had two major titles to defend: the Italian Open and the French Open. As usual, the important clay court season kicked off with the tournament in Rome. But things didn't go the way I had hoped. I breezed through the early rounds, but in the quarter-final against Mexico's Raúl Ramírez, it all went wrong before the match had even started.

On the way to the stadium, I realised I'd forgotten my badge, the player ID you get at every tournament. I figured it wouldn't be a problem since most people knew who I was. But no such luck. Two Italian police officers stubbornly refused to let me in. I tried reasoning with them while the crowd inside the packed arena was getting restless, shouting for us to start.

After an hour of back and forth, the officers finally shrugged and let me through, but by then I was furious and completely off my game. In tennis, playing angry doesn't work. You make bad decisions, get impatient when you need to stay cool. I lost in straight sets, and Ramírez went on to win the whole tournament, beating Vilas and Orantes on the way. I stayed mad for weeks, I really felt like that tournament should've been mine.

It's no secret that I can hold a grudge, so I promised myself I'd never play the Italian Open again. I stuck to that decision for two years, until the organisers offered me an appearance fee I just couldn't turn down.

That time, I made it to the final and faced local hero Adriano Panatta. The crowd made it very clear who they were cheering for. When an Italian plays in Rome, let's just say people don't mind bending the rules a bit to help the hometown favourite. The spectators started throwing coins at me, hitting me probably twenty-five or thirty times. And the noise was insane, especially during big points and when I was serving.

But this time, I wasn't going to fall into the trap, get mad and lose my focus. Instead, I calmly picked up the coins and slipped them into my pocket. At every changeover, I'd take them out and very deliberately drop them in my tennis bag. The crowd eventually thought it was funny, and in the end, the atmosphere and the match turned out to be great. Adriano was upset about the loss, but now he's a close friend, and we've laughed many times about that crazy day.

The biggest tournament for me in 1975 was of course the French Open in Paris. I'd won my first Grand Slam there the year before, and now I was back to defend it. The year before, I'd been the surprise package. This time, I came in as the favourite and top seed. So the circumstances were very different this time.

The ritual with the French perfume was repeated. I knew from the year before how much it meant, and I went out myself to buy it in town. After every shower throughout the tournament, I sprayed myself with it for luck. I could smell it everywhere I went, though in the end, it probably wasn't all that fresh once you started sweating. The whole routine became a kind of compulsion for me, and I'd go on to repeat it at future French Opens. And it worked.

I didn't drop a set on my way to the semi-finals. Everything was working, and I felt in great form. In the semis, I faced Panatta again, and we had a pretty tight match, but I won in four sets. Then it was time to defend my title, and I was up against Guillermo Vilas, who had barely lost a set either, except for a tough semi-final against Eddie Dibbs.

Vilas and I were good friends and had trained together many times. He was one of the first, like me, to hire a full-time coach, his being the former great Ion Țiriac. Oddly enough, once Țiriac started coaching him, Vilas never wanted to practise with me again. I have no idea why, it was probably something Țiriac decided on his own.

In the end, the final was pretty uneventful. I handled the pressure and won my second successive French Open title in three straight sets.

My focus now was on Wimbledon. I came in well prepared and felt I had a real shot at winning. I was seeded third, behind Jimmy Connors and Ken Rosewall, and I cruised through to the quarter-finals where I was set to face Arthur Ashe.

Then something happened, the sort of thing every high-level athlete knows all too well. You do something minor, something you've done a hundred times before, but suddenly it goes slightly wrong, and the consequences are enormous. The day before the match, I was practising at Queen's Club and slid on the grass to reach a ball, like always. The grass was damp, which made it easier to slide but harder to control. I felt a pull in the back of my thigh and knew right away I'd strained it. Luckily it wasn't bad enough to force me out of the tournament, but I was in serious pain during the match against Ashe. I managed okay for the first two sets, but after that it got tougher and tougher. Without the injury, I might've had a shot at beating Ashe, though probably not at winning the whole tournament, which he actually ended up doing. I still wasn't quite there yet on fast grass.

Instead, I took the opportunity to rest and enjoy some time at home with my family. My parents couldn't always travel with me to tournaments, so they usually chose either Paris or Wimbledon – never both in the same year, since they had to stay home and run the shop, which needed attention every day. But this time it was summer, and the shop was closed for vacation, so the three of us took the chance to relax as much as possible out on Resarö with my grandparents. Dad had launched our beautiful wooden boat earlier that summer, so everything was ready for some classic Swedish summer weeks. Finally, I got to enjoy Mum's home cooking with the whole family.

Before the US Open, Labbe had an idea: we'd stay somewhere secluded and do our own prep, far from everyone else. Or maybe he just forgot to book us a room. Either way, we ended up at a dump in Queens, near Forest Hills. Calling it a hotel would be generous, but at least we had the place to ourselves. I'm pretty sure that no one in Grand Slam history has ever stayed somewhere worse than we did that year.

If the accommodation was questionable, the matches were anything but. The tournament had been played on grass before, but this year it was switched to clay for the first time. I cruised through the early rounds, and in the fourth round I once again faced my old idol Rod Laver, beating him in four sets. The quarter-final against Eddie Dibbs also went to four sets and turned into a real showdown, with two sets going to tiebreaks.

Then I was ready for the big home favourite: Jimmy Connors. He was number one in the world, he had steamrolled everyone so far, and with the crowd behind him, he was the clear favourite to win it all. Still, I felt like I had a real shot in the semi-final.

It was a tight match and we both played great tennis. But the margins were on Jimmy's side, and he won 7–5 in straight sets. It could have gone either way, but he deserved the win. Everyone expected him to destroy Manuel Orantes in the final, especially since Orantes had just come through a five-set war with Guillermo Vilas. But that's not what happened at all.

Orantes won in straight sets. That's sport in a nutshell: you've got to deliver match after match, get the breaks, and recover if you lose your rhythm. It's the same for everyone.

So there was no US Open title for me that year either, though I didn't realise then that this tournament would turn into a kind of ghost haunting my whole career. It was a bit like playing Jimmy Connors between 1974 and 1976, when he won every single one of our matches.

In September, it was time for the Davis Cup play-offs, and our first match was against Chile on home turf in Båstad. Many people probably remember the protests against the Chilean military dictatorship, which made it uncertain for a long time if the semi-final would even be allowed to take place. I wasn't all that involved in the political side of things, I just wanted to play and win. But I could hear the chants echoing outside the arena and the sound of helicopters hovering over our heads.

I've since learned that the Swedish government actually wanted to cancel the whole event, but in the end it was decided that the matches would be played after all, but with a limited audience mostly consisting of journalists and officials, police officers and their German Shepherds. I've probably never had so many four-legged friends in the audience when I've played, neither before nor since.

Not having a home crowd to support us was, of course, a big disadvantage – a Davis Cup semi-final is meant to be a huge celebration. Even so, we won fairly easily and slowly started preparing for the final, which would be held in Stockholm a few months later. Hopefully there'd be a celebration then instead.

There was a break in the tournament schedule, and Helena and I finally got the chance to spend a few days together in Svärdsjö in Dalarna, where she lived with her family. Percy had arranged a rental car for me, an old Ford that unfortunately didn't have winter tyres. The roads were in rough shape with both the snow and ice, but I was determined to get there as quickly as possible, so I probably drove a bit too fast. I lost control in a left-hand curve, couldn't recover, and the car rolled off the road into a field.

I must've blacked out, because when I opened my eyes, I was hanging upside down in the seatbelt. I was totally groggy and had no idea what had just happened. Eventually, I managed to crawl out through the broken window, all the while worrying that I might have seriously hurt myself. When I got to my feet, still shaky, I saw the car. It was completely wrecked, except for the area around the driver's seat. If I've ever had a guardian angel, it was then.

But I was in a state of shock and still completely disoriented. I spotted a farmhouse in the distance and started walking towards it. With every step I took, I kept trying to check whether I'd really got out unscathed. Did my legs feel weird? Was my hand hurting? Could something be broken? It seemed impossible to survive a crash like that without a scratch. I also knew I was full of adrenaline and might not even notice an injury right away.

Eventually I reached the house and knocked. A family opened the door and immediately recognised me. Of course, they were wondering what on earth I was doing there. I doubt they understood much of what I said, I was probably just rambling in shock. But they called an ambulance right away. At the hospital, they examined me thoroughly, checked everything, ran X-rays, especially to make sure there were no internal injuries. The only thing they found was a small injury to my left thumb. Not a drop of blood had been spilled.

I was discharged shortly after and finally made it to Helena's

for a few days of rest. Even now, people in Svärdsjö still refer to
that curve in the road as 'Björn Borg's Bend'.

After the car accident I really needed rest. Thankfully, all the
major matches at the end of the year were being played in
Stockholm, so I didn't have to travel or stay in hotels. First
up was the Masters tournament in late November and early
December. Only the year's top eight ranked players were invited, and the prize for first place was $40,000, a huge sum at
the time, much more than what you'd win in a Grand Slam. I
played alright and managed to reach the final, but there I hit a
wall against my buddy Ilie Năstase.

I was disappointed, of course, but it was still fun to head
out with Ilie afterwards and enjoy Stockholm's nightlife. With
ten years on me, he was a bit of a mentor, and an undeniable
ladies' man. He adored beautiful women and had a real knack
for charming them. When Ilie was around, you didn't stand
a chance with the girls. In only a second he could swoop in,
charmingly say a few words, and suddenly everyone only had
eyes for him.

I remember a tennis tournament early in my career. I had
worked up the nerve to ask a girl down to the locker room, she
was going to wait for me while I showered, and then we'd go
out to dinner. But when I came out of the shower, there was
Ilie with my dinner date, and his hands were already under her
clothes. I stood there, furious, wearing nothing but a towel, and
shouted 'What are you doing?'

Ilie, being Ilie, just looked at me and said, 'I'm just warming
her up.'

That was the end of that. I didn't say much more, and in the
end, Ilie and I went out to dinner together instead.

*

The week before Christmas, it was finally time for the Davis Cup to be decided. Sweden's very first world final was set to take place at the Royal Tennis Hall. We faced a slightly favoured Czechoslovakia, who were clearly caught off guard by how tight-knit our team was. Captain Labbe had really brought us together into a squad that enjoyed playing and travelling as one. Now here we were, in the final, with the outcome completely up in the air.

In the fourth match, I faced Jan Kodeš, Czechoslovakia's top player. Now I had the chance to clinch the entire Davis Cup. Even though he was tough – he'd won Grand Slams in both Paris and Wimbledon – I knew deep down that I could beat him. And sure enough, I did. Straight sets. Victory!

I threw my racket in the air and jumped over the net, quickly shook hands with Kodeš, and ran straight to Labbe, who greeted me with a huge bear hug. Then he lifted me up, called the rest of the team over, and together they tossed me in the air at least ten times. I'd never experienced that kind of team spirit before.

When I finally landed on the ground again, we all agreed we had to toss Labbe too. I'd felt a mix of joy and awkwardness when it was me flying through the air, but not Labbe. You've never seen a bigger smile in your life. It was a huge triumph for him as captain, to win something as historic as the Davis Cup.

As always, the journalists came running onto the court, wanting to know how it felt. I did my best to answer when someone asked: 'Björn, can you describe how you're feeling?'

'No,' I replied.

And it was the truth. Some people are great at putting feelings into words, but sometimes you're so caught up in the moment that even trying is impossible. I was proud and happy about our Davis Cup win, but more than anything, I just wanted to go and celebrate with the team. And that's exactly what we did.

A few years ago, Patricia and I attended a big gala at the Royal Tennis Hall to celebrate the anniversary of that classic victory. It was a beautiful, memorable evening, and the whole team was back together again: Ove Bengtson, Birger Andersson, Rolf Norberg and me. Labbe's wife Rose-Marie was there too, along with their children and grandchildren. We all missed Labbe a lot that night. Of course we wished he could've been there with us. But in a way, it felt like he was – and in those unforgettable orange long johns.

9

The Kiss of Victory

A new chapter in my life began in Monte Carlo. Living there felt like being in a movie, or in one of those worlds you only read about in books. I was constantly overwhelmed by the thought: I actually live here now. It was just *wow*.

Our little family had moved into two apartments right next to each other, Mum and Dad in the bigger one, and me in a small studio I had to myself. The Estoril building complex was right on the Mediterranean, with a stunning view. On clear days, at certain times of the year, you could see all the way to Corsica. The glass windows were enormous and sometimes I forgot they were even there. More than once I walked straight into them before I finally got used to it. The apartments themselves were nice without being overly luxurious, but what really made them special was the view we had from the seventeenth floor.

After a few years, Guillermo Vilas moved into the same building, just one floor up, on the eighteenth. If we were both home, we spent a lot of time together. After training or playing at the Monte Carlo Country Club, he always wanted to go to Menton to eat at a particular Argentine restaurant. There was a lot of meat on the menu, which only made sense because meat was an Argentinian speciality.

My parents' shop was located right on the ground floor of our building, which was super convenient. But not long after, they bought a house about half an hour away, just over the border on the French side in Cap Ferrat. It was a great investment, because it was an exclusive spot and they liked having a garden and a quieter life. Still, they kept the shop running and drove back and forth every day.

My relationship with Helena had ended by then. It just slowly fizzled out as my tennis career took off. There was no drama, no messy break-up. It was simply clear that we were headed in different directions, and as I saw it, we were both relieved once we made the decision. I think it was probably a weight off her shoulders not having to deal with all the attention that constantly followed us both. There was never a moment of peace, and that kind of life didn't suit her at all. Honestly, it didn't suit me either, but I was so focused on tennis that I still put up with it.

At the same time, I was open to meeting someone new, someone I could build a long and hopefully stable relationship with. I felt like I needed that. Funnily enough, it was actually Helena who had introduced me to Mariana Simionescu, and we already knew each other from the tour. I thought she was special in a lot of ways and was immediately interested when we met at a tournament in Bournemouth in 1976. I knew she was from Bucharest, Romania, the same age as me, and a strong tennis player – she'd won the junior French Open two years earlier, in 1974.

A few weeks after we first met, we saw each other again, this time right before the French Open in Paris. And that's where things really started between us.

But before Paris, I went to Kailua-Kona, Hawaii, to play the finals of a WCT tournament. Not only was there big money involved in World Championship Tennis, and a different format compared to regular ATP events, but the match time was also unusual. I was set to play Ilie Năstase in the semi-final at 7.30 in the morning. The reason? They wanted it to air at a good time for the US mainland.

We couldn't even warm up properly. It was pitch dark, the sun hadn't come up yet, and there were no lights on the court. So Labbe and I just went for a walk. Ilie wasn't exactly a morning person, so I couldn't use that as an excuse, but still, I lost 6–4 in the fifth and final set.

I had been clearly ahead when Ilie started doing his thing. At one point, he literally jumped into the stands and started chatting up a girl. The crowd loved it and everyone was laughing, but both Labbe and I were going out of our minds. That kind of psychological warfare drove us nuts. He won that 1976 match in Kailua-Kona, but right then and there I promised myself: I'm never losing to him again.

The day after the loss, Labbe and I were supposed to fly to another tournament in the US, but I was in such a bad mood I cancelled. Instead, we decided to stay an extra week in Hawaii. We lived it up with boat trips, sunbathing, swimming, and always a drink in hand. That week completely turned things around. I think what we really needed was just to rest, and that time together brought us even closer. That week in Hawaii is one of my dearest memories of Labbe, something I really treasure. We were incredibly tight, and we stayed that way for years.

*

Before the French Open in Paris, I started getting jittery. Much to Labbe's annoyance, I called Mariana, who was also in Paris to play the women's tournament. It was actually my birthday, I was turning twenty. Most of the players on both the men's and women's tours stayed at the same Sofitel Hotel during the French Open. The rest of the year, we usually played at separate venues, so Grand Slams were the only real chance to meet.

Labbe thought my timing was terrible. He said I had no business getting distracted when I had a title to defend. But I didn't back down and I invited Mariana out to dinner to celebrate. It was a lovely dinner with candlelight and everything, and right away there was this easy, relaxed vibe between us. Inside, I had a strong feeling that something good was starting. I felt safe with her, it felt like it was just us two, even though we kept our separate rooms while in Paris. We made sure not to let anything interfere with our training, diet or sleep.

I lost a tough quarter-final to Adriano Panatta, who went on to lift the trophy that year. He remains the only player ever to beat me at the French Open – twice, actually. Mariana had already been knocked out of her tournament, which gave us a few extra days together before it was time to move on.

So Paris ended up being a success for me, even if not on the court. I felt great with Mariana, and by the time Wimbledon came around, I was in excellent shape. Even Labbe had softened a bit. He still thought I should devote every waking moment to tennis, but he could see how good I felt and sensed that something real was starting to develop between Mariana and me. In fact, it was his idea that she join us on the drive from Paris to London in our trusty Saab. Before that drive, Labbe and Mariana had only exchanged greetings, but during the long ride they got to know each other better, and there was a great vibe in the car.

We checked into the Grosvenor House in London, and now Mariana and I had a shared room. We'd made sure to arrive early enough to give me plenty of time to train and gradually adjust to the grass. Labbe knew everyone on the tour and lined up great players for me to practise with. We often did sessions that lasted over four hours a day. Meanwhile, Mariana trained with Labbe, who helped her develop her game.

I was seeded fourth, behind Ashe, Connors and Năstase. The tournament started off well, and I cruised through to the round of 16 against Brian Gottfried. For the first time, I decided to add an extra hour of serving practice on top of my usual training. Turned out to be a bad call. I won the match, but I strained an abdominal muscle in the process. The next day, I had to have injections just to get out of bed. It was brutal pain, and it kept up every morning for the rest of the tournament. I had to lean against the wall just to walk. Evenings were the worst; when the numbing meds wore off, the pain doubled. At times I wasn't sure I'd even be able to finish out the tournament, but despite everything I was in such good form that I kept winning, first against Vilas in the quarters, then against Roscoe Tanner in the semis.

In the final, I faced Năstase. I know I groaned a few times during the match, like some players do when they hit hard, but honestly it was just because of the stabbing pain in my abs. I kept my promise never to lose to Ilie again and closed out the third and final set, 9–7. After match point, I threw my racket higher than ever and put my hands over my face, like I couldn't believe it.

And I really couldn't.

Năstase hopped over the net and gave me a warm hug.

At last, I got to kiss the Wimbledon trophy! Maybe I was the first to do that, I have no idea. It definitely wasn't something I had planned; it just happened. I never kissed the trophy in Paris. Not in any other tournament, either. Only Wimbledon felt like the right moment, and that probably says something about how much those wins meant to me. And always falling to my knees, that was also always spontaneous.

A dream had become a reality: I'd won Wimbledon, at age twenty. And I hadn't lost a single set the entire tournament – something which has only happened one time since then.

10

Best in the World

Life couldn't have been better, with the success at Wimbledon and falling in love with Mariana. She had been incredibly supportive of me throughout the tournament, and everything felt right with her. The only downside was the abdominal injury, which forced me to pull out of Båstad that year. On the bright side, it gave Mariana and me the chance to fly to Bucharest and meet her parents.

Romania was behind the so-called Iron Curtain back then, a closed-off country under communist rule. But Mariana had good connections with the government because of her career as a professional tennis player. That meant we had no issues getting in and out of the country even though it was closed. Crossing the border to the West was something other people in the country could only dream of.

Mariana came from an ordinary Romanian family, and tennis was what had allowed her to travel abroad from a young age. The same went for Ilie Năstase. There weren't many tournaments held behind the Iron Curtain, and if you wanted to compete internationally, you had to travel. Tennis players, like other athletes, were seen as important ambassadors for their countries. For the communist nations the Davis Cup was especially important: its organisation into national teams was perfectly suited to propaganda.

Mariana and I finally got to enjoy some vacation time together, and she had the chance to show me her home country. We spent two amazing weeks on the Black Sea, visiting places like Constanța and Mamaia. The country was beautiful, and Mariana was the perfect guide. She was recognised everywhere, and we were welcomed warmly wherever we went. We also got to know the Romanian footballer Radu Nunweiller and his wife, and we would go on to spend a lot of time with them in the years to come.

After those summer weeks together, Mariana left Bucharest for good and moved in with me in Monte Carlo. We swapped my little studio for my parents' larger apartment, since they had moved to Cap Ferrat. But we still made regular visits to Romania to see family and friends.

Life in Monte Carlo suited us perfectly. It was a place where I could really relax and be myself in between all the travelling. We spent our days training at the Monte Carlo Country Club and our evenings dining out, always surrounded by family and friends. It was a lovely time. One of our favourite spots was the nightclub Chez Régine's, run by the unforgettable Régine Zylberberg, a true character in every sense. A Belgian-born French singer and nightclub queen, she called herself the 'Queen of the Night', and that title fitted her perfectly. She came alive after midnight and had business savvy like no one else, yet she was a warm and generous friend who always went the extra mile for those around her. She owned clubs all over the world and knew absolutely everyone who mattered. When she passed away in 2022 at the remarkable age of ninety-two, she was missed by many. Just imagine the wild stories she must have lived through over the years!

I'd made a lot of new friends in Monaco, including members of the royal family. When I had some time off, we'd get together for dinners at the palace, and I often played tennis with Prince Albert, now Prince Albert II of Monaco. When I needed serious training, there were two solid Monégasque players I could practise with: Michel Borfiga and Bernard Balleret. The whole royal family was tennis crazy. Who knows, maybe things could've worked out between Princess Caroline and me if I hadn't met Mariana. Then again, she was rumoured to have dated Guillermo Vilas for a while.

Monaco wasn't nearly as built-up back then. It was peaceful and quiet, although the construction boom started around the time we moved there. Since then, a lot has changed, and for many it probably doesn't have the same soul it did thirty or forty years ago. Things change, and it's easy to feel that things were better before.

Still, my parents made a point of staying connected to Sweden. They managed to buy the old summer home of Swedish business leader Curt Nicolin, an island property called Kättilö in the Gryt archipelago outside Valdemarsvik, a small coastal town in the southeast of Sweden. It was totally secluded and could only be reached by boat. As always, Mum and Dad had me in mind. On Kättilö, I could enjoy complete privacy whenever I was back in Sweden. For me, Kättilö and the house in Cap Ferrat were the two places that always felt like home.

Of course, we didn't get much time off as a family to spend at Kättilö. Mariana and I were constantly travelling, and my parents were busy running their shop in Monte Carlo. But we always made sure to go there at least once a summer and spend time together as a family. Those moments meant a lot to me.

My parents, who hadn't travelled much earlier in life, also got to see many parts of the world thanks to tennis. I brought them along to São Paulo, Brazil, a long and complicated journey. Labbe and I had flown ahead, and when we arrived at customs, they thought we were travelling salesmen trying to smuggle tennis rackets into the country for resale. That clearly wasn't allowed, and they decided right there on the spot to confiscate all my rackets, except one. They probably recognised me and just wanted to mess with me, or maybe make a buck off my gear. But for me, it was a disaster. There's no way I could play an entire tournament with just one racket. I tried to explain, but they weren't having it, they said that one was enough, that you don't use two rackets on the court at the same time, right? That rackets could break or that strings could snap were arguments they weren't buying. A few days later, they returned my rackets, but by then there was no time to restring them.

So when my parents arrived from Monte Carlo, I wasn't exactly in my best form. On top of that, they showed up late to my first match, which didn't help. They eventually found their seats in the VIP section, but by then, my game was completely off and I was incredibly frustrated. And then I took it out on them, which has always been my typical way of dealing with pressure. The ones I love and who are closest to me have been the ones to bear the brunt whenever something didn't work out. That's always been my pattern, from my time with Mariana all the way to Patricia today. I started gesturing towards my parents where they were sitting, and they immediately understood they needed to leave. It wasn't the first time it had happened, and it wouldn't be the last.

Once again my superstition was playing tricks on me. When things weren't working on the tennis court, I looked for outside reasons. It was especially unfortunate this time, since they'd come all the way to Brazil. But they came back for the next match, and things went much better. In the end, I won the whole tournament, despite the rough start.

Luckily, my parents knew how I was and didn't take it personally. I was genuinely happy to have them there. There was no one I'd rather celebrate a win with than Mum and Dad. And between matches, we got to spend some time together, even though during big tournaments, I mostly kept to myself and focused on training.

I also knew that if they couldn't attend a match in person, they were always watching on TV or listening on the radio. Sometimes Dad and Grandpa would take the boat out and fish for cod during big matches. Maybe they were nervous, or maybe it was just a convenient excuse to have a little time for themselves, but they always brought a radio along to follow the game. I can picture them now, sitting in silence, casting their lines, listening to the commentator describe the match, point by point. I hope they felt like they were with me anyway.

As summer drew to a close, it was time to head back to New York and once again try to win my first US Open title. I arrived as the reigning Wimbledon champion and second seed, right behind Jimmy Connors, who was again the favourite to win it all. In the semi-final, I faced Ilie, and once more, I kept my promise never to lose to him again. Jimmy had stormed through to the final without dropping a set. The only thing going against him, maybe, was that he'd done exactly the same the year before, only to lose in the end.

But that didn't happen this time. Jimmy played well and won

the match in four sets. I had at least made it to the final, which was a step closer than before, but I was still incredibly disappointed by the loss. When the year wrapped up, I was ranked number one in the world and named ATP Player of the Year. That had been one of my biggest goals: to become the best. It helped soften the blow a little, but I still hated losing.

11

A Raggedy Fox

I don't regret much, at least not during my tennis years, but when a US tennis league offered big money in 1977, I just couldn't resist. Looking back, I really should have. It prevented me from playing the French Open that year, the tournament that probably suited me better than any other. A missed opportunity, plain and simple.

The league was called World Team Tennis (WTT), built on the idea that American cities would field tennis teams to compete against each other, like hockey or basketball leagues. Each team had three men and three women, and five one-set matches were played in all sorts of combinations: men's singles, women's singles, men's doubles, women's doubles and mixed doubles. The rules were different too, you could be subbed out mid-match if the team or the player-coach thought you weren't performing. The season ran from June through August, with a break for Wimbledon – no top player was going to skip that. The best teams advanced to the play-offs.

Mariana and I moved to Cleveland, Ohio for three months and played for the Cleveland Nets, known today as the New Orleans Sun Belt Nets. The team was owned by Joe Zingale, an eccentric guy who also owned several radio stations in Cleveland. Many of the world's top players took part in the WTT circus. Martina Navratilova had been the star of our team before me, but once I joined, they couldn't afford us both.

The atmosphere and level of seriousness were nothing like on the regular tennis tour. It felt more like a spectacle. Our team didn't even make it to the finals. To be honest, winning in Team Tennis didn't mean that much to me. I wasn't thrilled when I won, and I wasn't that upset when I lost. The money had got to me.

It wasn't much fun for Mariana either, even though she played well. She had already begun winding down her own career and mostly travelled with me. Neither of us really enjoyed life in Ohio, and most of all it felt strange not to be in Paris for the French Open. I knew I would have had a great chance to win again, but instead we sat in Cleveland watching the final on TV. Guillermo Vilas beat Brian Gottfried. Not for one second could I stop thinking how mad I was at myself. 'What the hell am I doing here, in Cleveland?' I thought, over and over. When I saw Vilas later at Wimbledon, the first thing I said to him was, 'You should thank me for winning the French Open!'

How could I have chosen American money over another title in Paris? But things were different back then. We didn't obsess over records like players do today. We didn't think about it. Tennis wasn't as lucrative as people thought, either. Things were more day to day than how it is now. It created a great vibe among the players, a looser, more relaxed culture compared to today's professional machine with PR teams and branding experts pulling the strings. But that also meant our routines were more homemade and a little amateurish by comparison.

That's probably why the money in the US was so tempting. When I signed with Cleveland, Joe Zingale promised me that if I won Wimbledon during the WTT break, he'd send me two Corvettes to Monte Carlo. That was unheard of at the time. No one on tour talked about prize money or bonuses like that.

Labbe had kept his distance from Cleveland. We met up again at Wimbledon to start preparing to defend my title. It took him about five seconds to make his feelings clear about the American league. He was irritated and said I looked worn out. 'You look like a raggedy fox!' he said the moment he saw me.

At first, I didn't understand what he meant, but it was obvious it wasn't a compliment. I'd lost weight, was tired, run down. His concern about my form wasn't unreasonable. The question was whether there was enough time to get back into shape for the year's most important tournament.

I had started a new routine at Wimbledon that people began to notice and comment on: I didn't shave during the tournament, getting scruffier with each round. Only after the final would I clean up. It was one of those quirky rituals or superstitions that may seem odd, but which in big moments meant a lot to my mindset.

Wimbledon was celebrating its centenary that year, and the 1977 tournament would turn out to be important not just for me, but also for Mariana. She had her best Grand Slam showing ever, reaching the round of 16, where she unfortunately lost to Virginia Wade, who went on to win the whole thing.

For me, the tournament was significant on a personal level. I've already mentioned my first encounter with Vitas Gerulaitis in the Orange Bowl final in 1972. After that, we didn't cross paths that often, but after our semi-final match at Wimbledon in 1977, we became real friends.

The match itself was incredibly tough. Vitas had plenty of chances to win. Up until that day, neither of us had played better tennis. It became one of those classic Wimbledon matches. For a match to be called magical, both players have to be at their peak. The momentum has to swing back and forth, with impossible shots that surprise both opponent and crowd. And you should never know who's going to win until the last point is played. That's exactly what this match was.

Vitas and I were both quick, solid from the baseline. He constantly rushed the net, while I preferred starting from the back and moving in when the opportunity came. It went to five sets, but the third and fourth were where we both played our absolute best. We saved one impossible point after another. The crowd went wild.

I took the third set after a few perfect passing shots on my forehand, shots you only go for when you know you can pull off the impossible. But Vitas didn't back down. He opened the next set even stronger and held the lead to push it to a deciding fifth.

In the fifth, he again started stronger and forced me to save game points just to stay alive. Then, at 7–6 in my favour, with both of us holding serve until then, I hit a perfect lob on a passing shot. Vitas missed the volley on match point, and I won. It was one of the best matches of my career, and probably the most fun. But what I remember most happened the next day.

On Saturday, I went to the Cumberland Lawn Tennis Club in London for my usual pre-final training session. I don't remember who I was hitting with, but suddenly Vitas walked onto the court and greeted me cheerfully. No normal person does that the day after losing a huge match they were close to winning. But Vitas not only said hi and was friendly, he offered to train with me anytime, from that day on. Clearly, he had enjoyed the match as much as I had.

During all my years in pro tennis, I never met anyone with a bigger heart than Vitas Gerulaitis. He also had a brilliant sense of humour, he was a real comedian. That moment the day after our semi-final meant the world to me, and I know it meant a lot to him too. That's where a friendship began that would change both our lives.

On Sunday, 3 July 1977, I was back in the Wimbledon final, once again facing Jimmy Connors, who had just beaten the rising American star John McEnroe in the semis. Many thought Jimmy had a mental edge after winning several of our recent encounters, but I didn't feel that at all walking onto Centre Court. Most people probably expected the match to go a certain way: Jimmy would play aggressively, trying to hit winners. If he couldn't land his best shots, and I kept my errors low, I'd win. And that's more or less how it played out.

Jimmy took the first set, I won the next two. In the fourth, he served better and broke me at 4–2, but I lost my serve right away. We both had to dig deep to hold serve, but at 6–5, I lost my serve again, and Jimmy took the set.

I came out blazing in the fifth and raced to a 4–0 lead. I even had a break point for a near-unbeatable 5–0. Jimmy looked completely defeated, but then, out of nowhere, he hit a ridiculous drop shot. A shot no one would try under pressure, maybe at practice, and even then, you'd miss. But this one landed perfectly.

The crowd went nuts, and that lit a fire in Jimmy. He began clawing his way back while I was letting him back in mentally. He tied it at 4–4 and had the momentum. But I didn't panic. I focused on the next point, like always. Just as the match was tipping in his favour, I broke his serve and then served it out.

I'd defended my Wimbledon title. At twenty-one, I was still ranked number one in the world. Labbe was just as happy as I was, and this time he made it clear how impressed he was by both my game and mental strength. Maybe he'd even forgiven me for the whole detour in America.

But true to form, he was already looking ahead, next tournament, next win. That was Labbe. No resting on laurels. And maybe that was me too, always chasing the next challenge. Maybe this would be the year I finally won the US Open?

Mariana was thrilled after Wimbledon and was incredibly supportive. It was after this win that she more or less stepped away from her own tennis career and instead fully committed to supporting me in mine, taking care of all the big and small things I needed to be able to train, travel and compete. And maybe most importantly, she helped me feel good. She made it easier for me to relax between tournaments and matches.

Whatever happened to the two Corvettes I was promised? They did in fact show up at our door, but I sent them straight to my parents in Cap Ferrat. That's where there was space, time, and someone who would actually drive them.

After the Wimbledon win, I started earning even more money. Partly this was from the many matches I was winning, but more than half of it now came from sponsors and exhibition matches. My manager, Bob Kain at IMG, took good care of both me and my finances, always pushing me in the right direction. He had a strong business sense and was careful with contract lengths, so I wouldn't get locked into deals that might limit future opportunities.

My face ended up on all sorts of products, from headbands to jeans, tennis gear and running shoes. But also stranger things like clogs, toys, puzzles, figurines, sunscreen, cosmetics, soda, candy, even sewing machines. What mattered most to me was that none of it interfered with my time, especially during the key months of the season. From May to September, I didn't want to be disturbed. That was my time to lock in completely, to stay in my bubble and focus on delivering at the French Open, Wimbledon and the US Open. All my sponsors knew that, and they respected it. In return, I gave them pretty free rein to use my name and image however they liked. They weren't stupid. They knew that the more I won, the more valuable the deals became.

Family life in Monaco suffered because of all this. We rarely had the time together that we wanted. There were always more tournaments, more travel. Luckily, I still had my lifelong passion for boats, and I decided it was time to treat myself again. I wanted something moored in Monte Carlo harbour so we could easily head out for a swim, to get some sun, or just cruise along the coast.

It didn't stop at one boat, I ended up with two. Both were impulse buys from a local dealership just down the road from our apartment. If nothing else it was convenient, since they could keep an eye on the boats when we weren't around. They were fast Abbate motorboats, one seven metres long and one eleven, and if you're looking to burn through money quickly, high-performance boats are a great option. But honestly, they gave me a lot of joy, especially when time off was the biggest luxury I had.

Later on, Labbe took the smaller boat back to Sweden. I kept the big one, it was faster, more comfortable and handled rough water better. We used it as often as we could, and I loved the freedom of being out on the water. Sometimes it was just me and Mariana. Other times, my parents came along, and the goal was simply to find a great lunch spot, where we'd eat and drink well and stay for hours.

I have so many great memories from those boat trips. But there was one time when it nearly ended badly. One beautiful day, I suggested to Dad that we take the boat out on our own because it was a beautiful day, the sun was blazing, and the Mediterranean was almost perfectly still. I asked him if we shouldn't get away, just him and I, and have lunch in Antibes.

'Sounds great. When do we leave?' he replied, always up for something fun. We left Mum and Mariana in Monte Carlo, promising not to be too late.

We packed some rosé and cast off. It felt amazing to be out there alone with Dad, my closest friend. We enjoyed the sun and the sea, talked about everything, sipped some wine. Then we docked at a restaurant's pier and had an incredible seafood lunch, along with more rosé. It was such a good time that we didn't feel like going back just yet. So we decided to continue on to Saint-Tropez. By then it was early evening. We found a spot in the harbour, went ashore, wandered around, and eventually ended up at the nightclub Les Caves du Roy. We had so much fun that we completely forgot to check in with Mum and Mariana.

Back in Monte Carlo, they'd grown seriously worried and called the coastguard. They launched a full search, boats and even a helicopter. But we didn't notice any of it. We'd probably had too much to drink and either stayed on at the club or crashed in the boat for a while. When we finally came to at dawn, we headed home immediately.

I still remember that morning. It was the kind of morning only the Mediterranean can offer, sunrise, a gentle breeze and a sea like glass, glowing pale blue. But things weren't quite as peaceful back home. Mum was furious. She and Mariana had stayed up all night, waiting for updates from the rescue team. They were certain something had gone wrong, that we'd capsized or worse.

We'd been thoughtless and selfish, not even sparing them a thought during our night out. But that's often how it was when Dad and I were together, it was like time stood still. We always had so much fun. I still think of him often. And every time I do, I miss him terribly.

If there was one thing that frustrated me more than anything, it was injuries. Being in top form, only to be sidelined by illness or an injury that stopped me from performing. I often find myself thinking back to those moments when I was injured and couldn't play at my best.

Like in the lead-up to the 1977 US Open in New York. I was in great shape and spent a lot of time beforehand out at Vitas's place on Long Island. We'd fast become close friends, and I was often over at his house, which was beautifully situated in King's Point. Vitas's parents were originally from Lithuania, but both he and his sister Ruta were born in New York. All four of them lived together in Vitas's big house and spent a lot of time with each other, not unlike my own upbringing. That was probably when the thought first hit me: I wanted a house on Long Island too.

Ruta was also a solid tennis player, and even Vitas's dad, Vytautas, was involved in the sport. Mariana and I actually played a few mixed doubles exhibition matches against Vitas and Ruta. For the four of us, tennis was pure joy.

Vitas had a court on his property that was built to match the exact surface used at the US Open. When they changed venues and surfaces for the tournament – from grass to clay and then to hard court at Flushing Meadows in Queens – Vitas had his home court resurfaced to match. No detail was left to chance.

We trained hard, preparing for the tournament that was now just a few days away. But then, on the Sunday before the first round, we had the brilliant idea of going water skiing, to unwind, take our minds off tennis for a bit. Vitas had a small boat, and the weather was perfect, so it felt like the thing to do. Unfortunately, I fell badly and hurt my right shoulder. I had no choice but to go home and try to recover as best I could.

On the first matchday, I barely made it onto the court. The pain in my shoulder was intense. Somehow, I still managed to win both my first- and second-round matches, but in the third round, I had to retire and withdraw.

It was incredibly frustrating, and I beat myself up over it for a long time. I mean, how stupid do you have to be to go water skiing just days before the US Open?

12

Homecoming

L abbe couldn't let it go that I'd chosen to play Team Tennis in the US instead of the French Open. He kept bringing it up, harping on it, saying it had ruined things for me.

'What did I tell you?'

Even though I pretended not to care, deep down I knew he was right. But I had more money in the bank now, and that meant something, too.

Having him as my coach really was a luxury. If I had listened to him even more closely, I'm sure both my life and career would've gone in a different direction, probably with even greater success and for more years. But sometimes, you've got to let yourself have a little fun. At least that's how I saw it.

But now I'd made up my mind, after my Team Tennis adventure, 1978 would be my best year ever. I was going to map out a proper, serious schedule with Labbe. And this time, I'd listen more, since I had a bad habit of signing up for too many tournaments.

So I kicked off the season more motivated than ever. But it didn't start well. Everything felt shaky, minor injuries were getting in the way, even if they were nothing serious. An annoying issue with my little toe, for example, forced me to skip the Monte Carlo tournament. The toe healed, but the spring passed without any real matches. I was getting increasingly frustrated because I knew I was probably in the best shape of my life.

As May drew nearer, and with it the Italian Open in Rome, I started to feel slightly panicked about the whole situation. I still hadn't played any real matches yet. Maybe I'd have to swallow my pride and go back, despite the whole police incident three years earlier. They were offering a huge appearance fee.

I decided to play, and this time I beat Panatta in the final. That felt great, of course, but maybe even better was that I managed to win over the crowd in Rome. They started out throwing coins again, but by the end of the match, they'd swung around and welcomed me as the winner, even though I'd just defeated their hometown hero. But once again I said: never again, Rome. The city is amazing, but I'd had too many bad experiences there. When I'm playing tennis, I want to focus on that and nothing else. And this time, I kept my word. I never played there again.

When the French Open rolled around, I was burning for revenge after my American detour. I saw it as my most important tournament of the year, especially after the fiasco the year before. I didn't drop a single set the entire tournament, and I think I didn't lose more than thirty games in total across all seven matches. Vilas, for example, only managed to take five games off me in the final. After the match, in the locker room, I muttered to myself: 'I'm back!'

That's exactly how it felt. I could feel it in every part of me, I'd never played better. After Paris, I was eager to keep the

momentum going and defend my Wimbledon title. I felt unbeatable there, too, although I almost blew it in the very first
round against Victor Amaya. After that, things clicked. I didn't
lose a set from the round of 16 against Geoff Masters all the way
to the final against Jimmy Connors.

On the morning of the final, 8 July 1978, I woke up with the
feeling that no one could beat me. This time, I had the psychological edge, and the match played out pretty much as expected.
Jimmy played aggressively, often coming to the net, and I had to
find the passing shots to counter him. Aside from a shaky start,
everything went smoothly. I dropped just seven games in the
whole match and, less than two hours later, I was the champion.
I dropped to my knees, almost as if I was thanking the heavens.

After Jimmy and I shook hands and thanked each other for
the match, someone else approached me, three-time Wimbledon
champion Fred Perry. He said a few kind words, though I didn't
catch them amid the chaos. It was surreal to realise I'd matched
what he had done forty years earlier. It meant so much, especially since I'd been sponsored by Fred Perry and worn his name
on my clothes early on in my career.

Maybe now I could even dream of pulling off the near-
impossible: a *true Grand Slam*, all four majors in a single year. It
had become harder with the intense competition in men's tennis,
but I'd already won the French Open and now Wimbledon.
If I could win the US Open, I could go all-in and head to
Melbourne at the end of the year for the Australian Open.

Labbe was in an amazing mood after Wimbledon. He kept
telling anyone who'd listen that I was playing better than ever,
and that the biggest improvement was my serve. He'd worked
hard on the rhythm of my motion and getting me to toss the
ball higher. I'd always had a solid serve, but now it was on par
with the best in the game. It's the small details that make a big

difference, plus the will to grind them out over endless hours of practice.

I also wanted to play back home in Sweden, so I entered and won the Swedish Open in Båstad. That was my eighth singles title that year, and finally, I gave myself a break. We headed to my beloved Kättilö to relax with the family. Everyone was in a good mood, and the Swedish summer was absolutely glorious. I decided to rest all the way up to the US Open.

Well ahead of the tournament, Mariana, Labbe and I flew to New York. As usual, we stayed at the Roosevelt Hotel in Manhattan and trained at Vitas's place out on Long Island. Everything felt perfect. I was pumped, in top shape, and confident I'd be hard to beat. But there was always something weird when it came to the US Open, something strange happened every time. And this year was no different, although this time it had nothing to do with tennis or training.

One day, the hotel receptionist called up to our suite. A man on the line said some people were there to see me, it was 'my American mistress and our son'. I said I didn't have a mistress or a son, but they were let in anyway. A moment later, there was a knock at the door. I opened it and found a woman standing there with a young boy. The boy shouted, 'Pappa, Pappa!' I had, of course, never seen them before, but I let them in. The woman placed a tape recorder on the table to record our conversation. She pointed at me and said her son had waited so long to meet his father. Eventually I'd had enough and asked them to leave, and they did. But sadly, this wouldn't be the last time I'd see the woman and the young boy.

A few months later, at another tournament in the US, the same boy came running up again, calling out 'Pappa, Pappa!' I told the woman that if she kept harassing me, I'd have no choice but to report her to the police. I never saw them again after that.

Of course my tennis friends got wind of the whole thing and took every chance they could get to tease me, 'Pappa, Pappa!', which I didn't find funny, even if I knew they meant it as a joke. Mariana didn't like it either, she could be a little jealous, just like me. I was in the spotlight, and for her, it couldn't have been easy with all the girls constantly crowding around.

Preparation for the US Open continued, and now it was just a matter of staying healthy. I definitely wasn't getting back on water skis or doing anything crazy with Vitas again. But I never imagined it would be something as small and stupid as a blister on my thumb that would trip me up this time. It was almost worse than that damn little toe earlier in the year.

I had cruised through all my matches leading up to the final and was now set to face Jimmy Connors again. He'd knocked out John McEnroe the day before. All that was left was my final Saturday training session. Mariana, Labbe and I went out to Long Island to hit with Vitas. Afterwards, I still don't know exactly what happened, but by evening, my thumb had swelled to twice its normal size. It was probably caused by an old grip on one of my rackets. The blister had filled with fluid under the skin of my right thumb and was really painful.

Labbe was beside himself and immediately took the blame: 'Maybe I didn't check all the rackets closely enough. Maybe I didn't replace the grips in time.'

But of course, it wasn't his fault. Doctors came to treat the thumb, which by now was throbbing. They tried numbing it and even injected cortisone straight into the finger, but that only made it impossible to hold the racket. Then they tried shots in my arm. Still no improvement.

By Sunday, I wasn't sure I'd be able to play at all. In the end, I decided to give it a shot, but Connors played great and got his revenge for Wimbledon, beating me easily.

Still no US Open title. The curse was back, and I started thinking that maybe this had been the best shot I'd ever have at both the US Open and the Grand Slam.

The blister wound led to a long, drawn-out break, a forced pause I couldn't enjoy the same way I had enjoyed my summer rest. Instead of competing, I had to focus on running and other forms of training just to stay in shape. My goal was to be back in time for the Stockholm Open in November. It had been a strange year, being in top form but constantly held back by small, nagging injuries that cost me matches. It wore on my competitive spirit. Still, when I was on the court, I felt unbeatable. I never got tired, no matter how long or gruelling the matches were.

At the Stockholm Open, I faced John McEnroe for the very first time – extraordinary to think we'd never played before. He beat me in straight sets, and I was incredibly disappointed. So much for a homecoming celebration, and it came so soon after my US Open loss. That match marked the beginning of a long rivalry between us. We never faced each other on clay, the surface John liked least – otherwise, the results might have been different. But by the time I ended my career, we were even. We had played each other fourteen times and each of us won seven. That's how close it was between us.

There are definitely things I wish I hadn't done during my career. One clear mistake was something as stupid as posing for a photo, without thinking of the consequences.

Vitas and I had played a few exhibition matches, including one in Tel Aviv, Israel. After the matches, we were looking forward to some well-earned downtime and a chance to do a bit of sightseeing. We did everything tourists do: visited Jerusalem, walked in the footsteps of Jesus along the Via

Dolorosa, placed notes in the Wailing Wall, and took a trip to the Dead Sea.

And that's where we messed up. After our swim, a few Israeli soldiers came over to say hi. They said they liked tennis and knew who we were. They took photos, asked for autographs, and we chatted for a bit. Then, in the middle of all this, they suggested we try on their uniforms. Neither Vitas nor I were politically savvy, and before we knew it, we were dressed in their gear. Someone handed us a machine gun, and we posed with it for a few photos. We didn't think much of it at the time.

After our day off, we headed back to the hotel, then flew on to Paris. When we arrived at the Hotel George V, near the Champs-Élysées, the place was swarming with reporters, more eager than usual to talk to us. I remember turning to Vitas and saying: 'Something must've happened. I wonder what.'

As soon as we got out of the taxi, reporters rushed us, shoving microphones in our faces. Everyone wanted my reaction to the photos that had just been broadcast around the world. We had no idea what they were talking about, and they only seemed interested in my response. Eventually we realised the soldiers must've sold the fateful photos of us posing in their uniforms and with their weapons. We were quickly forced to understand that we'd caused a massive public outcry.

We managed to get past the press and locked ourselves in our room, deciding to keep a low profile for a while. We stayed inside for days, kicking ourselves for being so naive. When we finally saw the photos, it became clear why everyone was focused on me. The image had been cropped so that only I was visible.

Though I kept a low profile, the controversy raged on and I soon began receiving death threats. The first came from the Red Brigades in Italy, a terrorist group with close ties to others who quickly followed suit. I decided to head to the house in

Cap Ferrat and hired eight armed security guards: two stationed inside the house, six outside around the property. It was a completely surreal experience. I was terrified and barely slept for days. How could I have been so stupid, to pose for those pictures? Worse still, to hold a weapon?

Through some contacts, I eventually got a message to Yasser Arafat, the leader of the Palestine Liberation Organisation (PLO), who had enormous influence in the Middle East. They asked him if I should be worried for my life. After the conversation, Arafat issued a public statement saying that no one was to harm me.

Life could return to normal again. And I could play tennis, something I hadn't been able to do since the disaster with the photos. It had been an incredibly scary experience, how something so seemingly harmless could spiral so far out of control. I'd learned a hard lesson: when you're famous, you're always under scrutiny. Every careless decision can have serious consequences.

13

Tennis and Rock 'n' Roll

In the music world, you hear about global tours that can last for months, sometimes even years. Tennis is kind of the same. As soon as one tournament ends, another one's right around the corner. Every player has to plan their year carefully and pick which events to play.

For me, that meant I only played the Australian Open once, even though it's a Grand Slam tournament. From 1977 to 1982, the Aussie Open took place at the end of the year, and by then I usually wanted to wind down and spend time with my family after a long season, and recharge for the next year. A tennis season is packed with tournaments, and it's hard to find time off. Of course, you want to show up, for your sponsors and for the ATP tour, but the sport is tough and it takes a real toll on your body. Plus, Australia is far away. The one time I did play the Australian Open, in 1974, it just happened to line up with the Masters, which was also held in Melbourne that year.

Would I have flown to Melbourne if I'd had the chance to

win a real Grand Slam? Absolutely. If I had won the US Open, the temptation would've been huge. Only five players in history have ever pulled it off. The legendary Rod Laver is the only one to do it twice, 1962 and 1969. At the time when it could've happened for me, the Australian Open started in December and then went on through Christmas and New Year, finishing in January. So both I and some others decided to skip it. In recent years, the entire Australian Open has been moved to after the New Year holidays, and that's one reason why all the players participate in it now. Another, even more important reason, is the fierce fight for ATP points today. You have to play all the big tournaments, and it's also required because of sponsor contracts. Fortunately, the tournament dates are now better spread out over the year.

A lot of tennis players and rock musicians know each other, and we often got along really well. Our lives weren't so different – we were constantly travelling, often staying in the same hotels. The only real difference is we're up during the day and they're up at night.

Even though the US Open gave me a hard time, I've always had a special connection to New York. There's a pulse there you just don't feel anywhere else. Vitas and I used to hang out a lot when we were both in town. Sometimes he'd bring his friend, guitarist Peter Frampton, and we'd go out to eat or grab a drink. Other times, Vitas and I would catch one of Frampton's concerts at Madison Square Garden. Frampton loved tennis, actually, a lot of musicians did. We'd sometimes even be playing at the Garden ourselves, so we'd run into each other there pretty often.

A lot of times it was just coincidence, being in the same city at the same time as certain musicians. You never knew where or when you'd bump into each other again. In Sydney, we met a young band who had just broken through, they were called The Police. In Dubai, I ran into Tina Turner. We actually met several times, but especially early in her solo career, when she was going through a rough patch after leaving her abusive marriage with Ike Turner. A couple times, she came to our hotel, sat down at the piano and just played, no pressure, just being herself. It was incredible to sit there in the same room and listen.

In Los Angeles, we hung out with the guys from Aerosmith a lot. They loved throwing parties and doing private shows. In Miami, I remember a great night with Paul Simon, who was in town for a concert. We had dinner and ended up out at a club until the early morning. Of course, whether I joined in the nightlife or not always depended on whether I was still in a tournament. No way I was hitting nightclubs if I had matches to play. Partying at night and playing tennis in the morning? That's just not doable if you want to be one of the best.

Usually, it was just a couple of days, or even just hours, between a final and heading off to a new city and a new tournament. Just like musicians, right after a show, everything gets packed up and off you go to the next stop. People say Bob Dylan is on a 'never-ending tour'. That's exactly what it feels like in the middle of a tennis season. You wake up, eat breakfast, warm up, train or play, eat again, train or play some more, wind down, crash in a hotel room that looks just like the last one. And the next day, the same thing all over again. It might sound glamorous, but it quickly turns into a routine that's hard to understand if you haven't lived it.

One night, Vitas and I ran into Roger Waters from Pink Floyd and decided to grab dinner. Roger loves tennis and plays whenever he gets the chance. Since we were all staying at the Beverly Hills Hotel, we agreed over dinner to hit the court together the next morning. When we left the restaurant, Roger headed back to the hotel to get some sleep, and Vitas and I were supposed to do the same. But at the last minute, we detoured to a bar around the corner for a nightcap. That turned into more than one drink, and soon enough we were out clubbing, having a blast. It got a bit awkward when we stumbled back towards the hotel and saw Roger, already out on the tennis court, fully dressed and practising his serves. Vitas and I had no choice but to crawl into bed and sleep it off.

Vitas hung out with a lot of sports-crazy musicians and was always dragging me to concerts. It could be football fanatic Rod Stewart or Elton John, who used to travel with his own tennis coach. Vitas was also a solid guitarist. He had real talent and even took lessons from none other than Carlos Santana, who would drop by his place from time to time. Vitas's mum, Aldona – everyone on the tour called her Mrs G – sometimes complained about his obsession with music. She said I was the only one who could get him to train seriously. With the other players, he'd show up on court blasting music.

There's a very special memory hanging on the wall at home from the days we used to hit the clubs in New York. The big one, of course, was Studio 54. I loved that place, it was in an old theatre right in the middle of Manhattan, near Central Park. Huge dance floor, big balcony, massive bar, and lots of little corners where people could sneak off and do ... whatever they wanted. All kinds of celebrities were there, hot musicians, artists, business types, models, dancers, you name it. Vitas and I went there a lot. One time, even my mum, dad, grandma and grandpa came along. As crazy as that sounds, it somehow felt totally natural. I wasn't embarrassed, they had a great time. Well, except maybe my grandma, who thought the music was too loud and there were too many drugs.

A lot of people thought Vitas and I looked alike, and he definitely used that to his advantage when he could. He was nicknamed 'Broadway Vitas' because he was such a showman and a regular on the nightlife scene. He always picked up the tab, no matter how big the group. One year, he supposedly had the third-highest American Express bill in the world, which says something about his lifestyle.

For me, going to Studio 54 wasn't about partying hard. It was more like a wild little break in an otherwise structured life. It has to have been one of the craziest scenes I've ever seen, even more outrageous than a Broadway show, because everyone looked so unique. You never had to wonder if it would be fun, it always was.

Tennis still came first. But if I had a night off and wasn't training the next day, I might let myself have a few beers. I was kind of a regular there, but I barely knew anyone's name. Vitas and, later, McEnroe were the social ones. They knew everyone and would introduce me to them all.

Andy Warhol was someone it was easy to like. He was strange in that he was both super shy and super bold at the same time. I went with him a few times to his place, The Factory, kind of a mix between a private club and his personal art studio. If there's one thing I regret, it's that I never said yes when he offered to paint my portrait in that characteristic style that only he could do. He gave me a few of his works, but I've only kept one: one of his classic Campbell's Soup Cans, with a note that says 'To Björn from Andy Warhol'. It's that painting that hangs on my wall at home, a reminder of those years. A time I wouldn't trade for anything.

It's kind of funny – some of the musicians I used to hang out with back in the '70s and '80s are still out there, doing their own kind of senior tour, just like I was. One time, Mats Wilander and I were in LA for a senior tournament, and we got invited to a studio where the Rolling Stones were recording a new album. One afternoon, we were just hanging out, leaning over Keith Richards's shoulder as he messed around at the mixing desk. Stuff like that stays with you.

I spent a lot of time with the members of the Stones over the years. One night after the 1977 Masters, Labbe and I planned to have a quiet night out. We ended up at Studio 54 anyway, and bumped into Mick Jagger and some of his friends. We all went back to Mick's place for an afterparty. I remember sitting on the couch laughing as Labbe tried to show Mick some new dance moves. It was hilarious. Mick was in a fantastic mood that night, totally relaxed and just being himself.

A while later, I was woken up at my hotel late one night by Labbe. We had an agreement that he would handle all my calls, but this time he thought I should pick up. It was Mick's then-wife Bianca Jagger. She was a bit bored and asked if I wanted to come over. I didn't think too long about that one. I got dressed and we went out partying.

One rock musician with a real connection to tennis is Lars Ulrich, drummer for Metallica. His dad was Torben Ulrich, the charismatic Danish tennis player who refused to play matches in the morning and had a lot of strings to his bow. He was a great tennis player, but he also devoted himself to writing, making films and playing music. And with his long hair and beard, he definitely stood out. I first met him in 1971 in Kingston, Jamaica, when we played doubles together. He was actually the first person who introduced me to using meditation and yoga as part of training.

Lars was often with his dad, so tennis was in his blood. I'm always happy when I run into him.

The funny thing is that I rarely crossed paths with Swedish musicians or artists, even ABBA, who were also famous all around the world and on the road as much as I was. The only time I met them was once in their recording studio back home. I never saw them live, which is a shame. The only Swedish musician who really became special to me was Ted Gärdestad. He was one of Sweden's top tennis prospects from my age group, born in 1956, just like me. When we were fourteen, I was ranked number one and he was number three. We both became teenage idols, just in totally different ways. He was a singer and songwriter, his debut album produced by none other than Björn and Benny from ABBA.

Ted was an amazing guy, kind, incredibly talented, both in tennis and in music. It was like everything he touched turned to gold. One of his songs is called 'Helena'. He wrote it for Helena Anliot, then his girlfriend, who also happened to be my first love. Ted and I tried to stay in touch for a long time, but it got harder after he left music and joined a cult. I asked his brother Kenneth a few times if there was anything I could do, but unfortunately Ted slipped deeper into mental illness. The last time I saw him was just before he passed. I was parking at the Nordiska Kompaniet garage in Stockholm on my way to a meeting and saw him standing outside the department store. It was ten in the morning, so I figured he was just waiting for it to open. I was running late, so I just waved and said hi.

When I came back around six that evening, he was still standing in the same spot. I went up to talk to him, but he was completely unreachable. It broke my heart. Not long after that, he chose to end his life, and it all felt so tragic and wrong.

My interest in music started early on in my childhood in Södertälje, listening to Radio Luxembourg on a little radio. It broadcast in English, something exciting and exotic for many people my age. I had a mic next to it so I could record onto my little portable cassette player, usually with interruptions like: 'Björn, dinner's ready!'

A few years later I got my own record player. The first albums I owned were by the Beatles, Elvis and the Swedish band Hep Stars. I never saw the Beatles live, and I've never met any of them, but John Lennon's songs have always touched me deeply. That's why it felt right to play his song 'Woman' at my wedding to Patricia.

Some of my best memories in life are tied to music, even though I never played an instrument myself. I love music, whether I'm at a concert or just listening at home. Music calms me down more than silence ever could.

PART THREE

Grand Finale (1979–1981)

14

The Winning Machine

When I look back on the most successful years of my career, 1978 to 1981, strangely, the memories are fewer. I can hardly tell one year from the next. It was just tennis, tennis, tennis, around the clock. As usual, I trained four hours a day, travelled, played matches, stayed at one hotel, then moved on to the next. Eat at the restaurant, get a massage, take a shower, go to sleep, wake up for breakfast, then it was time for another training session. I was never picky about food or service. I eat pretty much anything and I've always been an early riser. But during tournaments, I absolutely needed a cool, dark room to sleep in.

It was one match after another. Win after win. As soon as I won a match, my eyes were already on the next one. If I won a tournament, my focus instantly shifted to the next. Every Grand Slam win just made the next one feel even more important.

That's how it went, non-stop, at a crazy pace. I coped with all the attention from fans and the press by keeping a low profile.

I never enjoyed the spotlight much and I had no interest in putting my personal life on display. For me, standing in front of cameras and talking at press conferences was torture, I avoided it as much as I could. It wasn't the attention itself that bothered me, people were generally kind and meant well, but it was harder with certain journalists. Some of them asked the same questions over and over again and tried to dig up stories that weren't even true. That's what really drained me.

The fans were different. Many were devoted, and I wanted to give them as much as I could, but even there, I had to start setting boundaries. I wanted to focus on playing my best tennis and spending time with my family and friends.

Was I able to enjoy my success? Yes and no. In one way, it gave me energy and a hunger to win the next match. I did take a moment to enjoy each win, but then I quickly moved on. Same with every point, I was always looking ahead. If I lost a point, I let it go immediately and focused on winning the next. It was the same with every ball – if I lost one, I immediately let it go and focused on winning the next. That ability to move on was my mental strength. Like after a perfect passing shot or a winning volley, I'd enjoy the feeling for a split second, then turn my attention to the next ball.

I was still a sore loser. I could sulk for ages and promise myself I'd never lose again, especially not to certain players. I hadn't forgotten my vow to never lose to Ilie Năstase.

The crowd wasn't just drawn to the game or the players any more. Now the tension between us had become part of the entertainment, and it was one reason tennis was booming. The rivalries and drama created headlines. First there was my battle with Jimmy Connors, when we were fighting for the top spot in the rankings between 1977 and 1979. Then came John McEnroe, challenging both Jimmy and me for the number one spot. Jimmy's playing style was more like mine, while John was a classic serve-and-volley guy. Off court, they had completely different personalities.

Around 1979, some sort of unique relationship started forming between the three of us. But in those early years, Jimmy and John were my rivals more than my friends. It wasn't until the senior tour in the '90s that a real friendship grew between us, a warm and genuine one that's lasted ever since.

But back then, during our playing years, Jimmy and John also had a rocky relationship with each other. In the beginning, Jimmy didn't even like me much, either as a player or a person. The first time we'd met was in the semi-finals at the Royal Tennis Hall in 1973. He later told me that everything about me annoyed him, my appearance, my mannerisms, even the way I walked. But he accepted me somehow, and it blew over pretty quickly.

With John McEnroe, it was different. He burst onto the scene at Wimbledon in 1977, seemingly out of nowhere. Jimmy barely managed to beat him in the semis, this young slugger from New York. The fact that both were American made their dynamic even more interesting. At first, Jimmy was only mildly irritated, like you'd be with a cocky teenager – which John actually was. But around 1978, things escalated. It became clear John wasn't just some flash in the pan, he was seriously challenging Jimmy's dominance. The Americans have always cared about hierarchy, who's ranked highest in the world, but this was also about who was number one in the US. That was tough for Jimmy. The competition at home was fierce.

They grew more and more annoyed with each other, and I, having got to know them both, somehow ended up playing the middleman. I was the calm and collected one. Whenever one of them started acting up, I was there to calm things down. I think they got used to me being the buffer between them, maybe they even liked it, because it allowed them to keep acting out. That was fine by me. I liked them both equally.

After I'd spent Christmas and New Year with Mariana and the family, the 1979 season kicked off. I was in good shape and went to the US to play a couple of tournaments: Richmond and New Orleans. While we were there, we also ramped up the search for a house. We wanted a place of our own on Long Island, just outside New York.

In Richmond, I faced John McEnroe again in the semi-finals. I was in real trouble – he had three match points against me in the final set – but I somehow managed to claw my way back and win. When we shook hands after the match, it was clear John was devastated by how things had flipped. I was unusually satisfied. It was sweet revenge after losing to him at the Stockholm Open the previous autumn.

After the semis, Labbe and I went back to the hotel to get ready for the final against Vilas. As soon as we arrived, I realised I'd forgotten my shoes at the arena. Being superstitious, I obviously wanted to wear the same pair in the final, so Labbe kindly offered to go back and get them. It was tough for him to get in, everything was locked and shut down, but Labbe doesn't give up easily. He eventually tracked down someone who got hold of a janitor who let him into the locker room. To his surprise, the lights were still on, and there was John, sitting alone. He was deep in thought, clearly going over every detail of the match he had just lost.

Labbe, always thoughtful, asked if he was okay, but John didn't even respond. When Labbe came back with the shoes, he told me John had been so lost in his thoughts he didn't acknowledge him at all. I instantly knew what he must've been thinking about, sitting there by himself. Outwardly our rivalry looked fierce, but despite all the intense matches, we had huge respect for each other.

I won the final against Vilas – it was my first title of the year and the fortieth singles title of my career. I was on a roll. But as always, the celebration was short-lived. New Orleans was next, with pretty much the same field. I faced John again, this time in the final. He'd been on his best behaviour in the previous tournaments, but maybe that loss from the week before was still haunting him, because now it was like the demons had taken over. He went completely nuts, like someone had let him out of an asylum, as we used to say. It wasn't fun for anyone, not for him, not for me, and definitely not for the crowd. But we kept playing, and I was up 4–1 in the final set. I just wanted to finish the match and get out of there. Then he had another meltdown, yelling, smashing his racket, muttering, complaining about every call.

I walked up to the net and motioned for him to come over. He must've thought I'd lost my mind. Why would I call him over? But he trudged up in that trademark way of his, and I calmly said: 'John, it's only a game.'

It was advice I could've just as easily given myself. And maybe I shouldn't have said it, because from that point on, the match turned. He saved three match points on his serve and eventually won. Still, I think that's when I earned John's respect. Maybe that was the moment our lifelong friendship really began.

New York had always held a special place in my heart, but so did Las Vegas, which I liked visiting with my family during those years. The main reason was that I had one of the best endorsement deals of my career, with the luxury hotel Caesar's Palace. They hosted an ATP tournament called the Alan King

Tennis Classic, which I played several years in a row. It offered solid prize money.

I won it back-to-back in 1979 and 1980, and as part of my deal, the hotel always kept a suite ready for me whenever I wanted to come to Las Vegas. Travelling there was made easier thanks to my contract with Scandinavian Airlines, which meant I always got quick and convenient flights around the world. Whenever I had the chance, I'd bring my parents, my grandparents or Labbe along to enjoy the lavish shows featuring stars like Liberace, Ann-Margret and Sammy Davis Jr. The performers were always generous afterwards. We'd get to go backstage, say hello and sip champagne.

One of the biggest milestones for Mariana and me was when we finally found our dream house, in Sands Point on Long Island. Spending more time in the US had become important to us, especially for me, since I loved being in New York. It had a pulse that was the opposite of how I'd previously lived my life. Plus, a lot of tennis tournaments took place on the American continent, so it made sense to have a home base there. Vitas was the perfect training partner, and I knew I wanted to live close to him.

The dream home we found after our long search was a large, newly built house by the water that we instantly fell in love with. The owner probably overcharged me, but I didn't want to risk losing it. We took a walk around the property on some side roads while he kept rambling about numbers and how many other interested buyers there were. Eventually, I couldn't take the sales pitch any more, so I made a generous offer above the asking price, and the house was ours.

The place was incredible: fifteen rooms spread over three floors, massive windows, a huge pool. Even by today's standards, it was a one-of-a-kind home. Best of all, it was only a thirty-minute drive from Vitas's house, where he lived with his parents and sister. I was really looking forward to training more with him and spending more time together. Vitas had the same drive I did when it came to training. Sure, people sometimes criticised him for not being serious enough, but when we trained together, I saw just how focused he could be. After all, he was a top-five player in the world for a long time.

Mariana and I absolutely loved the new house. We were both private people, and we liked staying home. My parents came to visit now and then, sometimes bringing my grandparents along too. It was so lovely living just outside the city but still being close to Manhattan, with its nightlife and celebrity scene. Vitas and I would take his silver Rolls-Royce Corniche convertible into the city and roll up to Studio 54, hand the keys to the valet, and watch the crowd as we walked in. But tennis was still everything, so during that period, I kept my clear distance from alcohol, drugs and wild late nights.

New York had more to offer than just nightclubs and parties. Ice hockey had once meant as much to me as tennis, and Madison Square Garden was the place to watch top-tier NHL games. I went as often as I could, many times with Vitas. We also spent time with Franz Beckenbauer and his wife. He was nearing the end of his career and playing for the New York Cosmos. 'Kaiser Franz' had been a superstar in soccer and is still considered one of the greatest of all time. Pelé was also in New York a lot after wrapping up his legendary career with the same club. We had dinners together. He was always a fun guy to be around.

Then came Europe and the clay court season. It was now 1979, and I had several major titles to defend. The first big tournament was Monte Carlo, where I beat Vitas in the final. That victory kicked off an incredible winning streak for me. In Paris, I won my seventh Grand Slam title, and after just a few days of rest, I headed straight to Wimbledon to defend my title there as well.

But Wimbledon started off rough. Right from the early rounds I had to fight hard to get through, especially in a five-set battle against Vijay Amritraj. Still, I made it to the final, where I faced the left-handed, big-serving Roscoe Tanner. After I'd beaten Jimmy Connors in the semis, most people probably saw me as the clear favourite to win my fourth straight title.

The final was tight and high-quality. Tanner won a crucial first-set tiebreak, and after that, the match swung back and forth until it came down to a fifth set. All throughout the match, it felt like Roscoe had the upper hand. I struggled to break him, his serve was just that strong. But in the fifth set, I broke him right away and held the lead until I was up 5–4. Now it was my serve, and I just needed to close it out. I raced to 40–0 and had three championship points, but I couldn't convert a single one. Maybe I got a little sloppy, but I just couldn't finish it. After that, I did what I always did: I shut everything else out, focused completely on each point, and finally served out the match. Tanner hit the next ball into the net, and on my fourth match point, I clinched my fourth straight Wimbledon title.

I dropped to my knees, but quickly got back up, raised my arms, and looked straight up at the players' box where my mum, dad, Labbe and Mariana were all jumping for joy. It wasn't the most physically draining match I'd ever played – it only lasted a little over two hours – but mentally it was a huge challenge. Probably because there was so much to lose. Labbe said afterwards that I looked more relieved than happy, and I think he was right.

Then something happened after the match that caught me completely off guard, in the best possible way. Later that evening, I got to meet the one and only Muhammad Ali, who congratulated me on the win. There are photos of us together – he's holding a tennis racket, and I've got a giant boxing glove. The whole room changed when he walked in, his charisma was unbelievable. Meeting him in person, and hearing what he had to say about me, was just overwhelming. He was the greatest of them all.

Still buzzing from Wimbledon, I went back home to Kättilö, but the vacation didn't last long. More tournaments were lined up, and that year, my sights were set firmly on winning the US Open. As part of my prep, I played the Canadian Open in Toronto, where I faced off against several younger players on the rise, like the Frenchman Yannick Noah and the Czech Ivan Lendl. In the final, I beat John McEnroe in straight sets without too much trouble.

That was the year the US Open changed its surface again, this time to hard court. The tournament had previously been played on green clay, which behaved a bit like hard courts, though it was faster and more slippery than the red clay in Europe. But now it was the real deal, proper hard court. Everything went well up until the quarter-finals, when I faced Roscoe Tanner again. He was definitely hungry for revenge after Wimbledon, and maybe that's why I ended up in a deep hole I couldn't climb out of. I lost the final set in a tiebreak. Once again, I hadn't managed to win the US Open, and my shot at a true Grand Slam went up in smoke.

After the match, I went straight out to Long Island to lick my wounds. It was a brutal loss in every way, and I couldn't wrap my head around why things always seemed to fall apart at the US Open, when I could win just about everything else. When I couldn't find a logical explanation, my superstitious side started to take over, and soon all kinds of strange theories were swirling around in my head. It became a vicious mental cycle, and I knew I had to find a way to break out of it.

Then something odd happened. Out of nowhere, a woman, some kind of medium, reached out to me, right when I was in the thick of all that overthinking. I'd always been curious about the spiritual side of things, and maybe my superstitions were part of that. Maybe she knew that and figured I'd be an interesting person to work with. Or maybe it was just a coincidence.

'Why not?' I thought. 'It can't hurt.' Maybe she could help me make sense of all the thoughts in my head, maybe even explain why I could never win the US Open.

We ended up meeting about ten times. She always came out to the house on Long Island. We'd sit across from each other and just talk normally, like any other conversation. No crystal balls or tarot cards like you might expect. The first time we met, it felt like she was testing me, checking if I could handle hearing whatever she had to say. Some people don't want to be told their future, but I was curious. I wanted to know everything.

After each time we met, I felt this strange sense of calm, even when she told me things that were hard to hear. I figured it was better to know than not to know. That way, I could use my willpower to steer things in the right direction. Do everything I could to prevent things from going wrong in my life. There were plenty of good things ahead, but also some really tough ones. She was a pro, she gave me the heavy stuff in small doses, so I'd have time to take it all in.

And everything she said came true. She predicted my business ventures would fall apart. She said Mariana and I would have problems. But she also said I'd have children in my life. She told me the stars were never aligned for me at the US Open, and that I'd never win there, and I never did. It was a bit eerie how accurately everything turned out, but it left me wanting more, and I actually ended up working with her for the next three years.

One of the more encouraging predictions was that the period between May and July would be to my advantage. That couldn't have been truer – just think of all the Grand Slam titles I won in Paris and London during those months. She said that's when I was at my happiest and most at peace. Maybe it had something to do with me being born on 6 June. Even now, I struggle with the dark months. They get me down. And I still wonder sometimes: was that the reason I never won the US Open? Because it was held later in the season?

In September 1979, I travelled to Palermo, Sicily, where an ATP tournament was being held for the first time ever.

Gino Marchese, the tournament director, also worked for IMG in Italy. He'd been trying to convince me to come for quite a while, but I hadn't been very keen. To be honest, I was nervous, I kept thinking about the mafia in that area. Probably an irrational fear, but I'd seen too many gangster movies, and they'd definitely coloured my view of Sicily.

Gino assured me there was no chance the mafia would have anything to do with the tournament, and eventually, I agreed to come. But as soon as I boarded the plane, I had a bad feeling. I couldn't put my finger on it, but something just felt off. And sure enough, the flight there was a nightmare. The turbulence was so intense that people started panicking, screaming, they really thought the plane was going down.

Luckily, we landed safely. And the tournament itself went well, right up until the final, where I was playing the Italian, Corrado Barazzutti. I was up two sets to love and 4–1 in the third when it started to rain. Normally, that would mean a delay.

But this time, I had a private jet waiting for me after the match, I was supposed to fly straight to London for a scheduled ad campaign. Barazzutti, of course, wanted to stop and resume the next day. And once he realised I had a tight schedule, he became even more determined. I walked up to the net and politely asked if we could at least play a few more games. Eventually, he agreed, and I was able to wrap things up quickly and win the match. Still in my tennis clothes, I went straight to the airport and landed in London a few hours later, with great memories of Sicily and nothing strange having happened. I slept like a rock that night and didn't wake up until late the next morning.

When I turned on the TV, BBC News was on. One of the lead stories was about Sicily. Several people had been murdered in Palermo. I called Gino right away. 'What happened?' I asked. 'Was it the mafia?'

He hesitated a moment before answering. I practically yelled into the phone: 'You promised nothing would happen with the mafia!'

He calmly replied, 'I promised nothing would happen during the tournament. And nothing did. But maybe they had other business that got postponed because of the event. Who knows?'

If Palermo ended up being a little too dramatic for my taste, the next trip more than made up for it. I was headed to Japan to play the Tokyo Indoors. I was really looking forward to it, it was going to be a mix of tennis, sponsor events, and time with my family. Japan was an important country for me. I had a sponsorship deal with Seibu, a major department store chain with locations all across the country, so I made it a priority to play every tournament I could there. I usually went twice a year, and on one of those trips, Mariana and I were even granted an audience with the Emperor of Japan. That kind of thing is incredibly rare, just getting inside the palace was a huge honour. The meeting was brief, but I'll never forget it. It felt truly special.

That year, my mum and dad came along. I figured they'd appreciate visiting a part of the world they'd never seen before. On the first day, as usual, I took my dad to the courts for practice, and my mum headed off to Seibu to do some shopping. As soon as she walked into the store, ten assistants showed up to help her out. The idea was that they would carry her bags as she shopped. The only problem was, she had forgotten her wallet. The only money she had on her were a few bills in her pocket. Still, she tried to keep her cool and hoped everything would work itself out.

The assistants suggested she start in the jewellery department and brought out little red silk cushions for her to rest her hands on while trying on rings. My mum is a very down-to-earth person, and on top of not having much money on her, she also had chipped, garden-worn nails from working in the yard right before the trip.

She ended up having to wriggle her way out of the jewellery section and head for the kitchenware department instead. Luckily, there was a sale on big, beautiful plates that she could actually afford, and the assistants finally had something substantial to carry. But she found the whole situation so embarrassing that for a long time she couldn't even talk about what had happened in Tokyo without blushing.

After I finished the tournament, we travelled to the amazing cities of Osaka and Kyoto, where we were treated like royalty everywhere we went. Japan is such a fascinating country, so full of culture and history. For two nights, we stayed in a traditional Japanese home, sleeping on the floor and eating on mats with our legs crossed. The food was probably fantastic, but I don't think anyone in my family really knew how to appreciate it like we should have. As soon as we left, we headed straight for a hamburger joint and enjoyed what felt like the best meal we'd had in ages.

One of the most special memories I have from the end of 1979 was being named the BBC Overseas Sports Personality of the Year, now called the BBC World Sport Star of the Year.

That one really meant something to me. Normally, I didn't care much about awards like that. I was more focused on winning matches and tournaments – the trophies themselves I often left behind at the hotel when it was time to move on.

I was reminded of the award recently, when the pole vaulter Armand Duplantis won it in 2024 and the media mentioned that no Swede had received the honour since 1979, when I had gotten it. That put it all in perspective.

Still, there are a couple of trophies I've kept over the years that really mean something to me, besides my Wimbledon cups, of course. One is from when I was voted Swedish Athlete of the Century in 2000. The other is a challenge trophy I once received from Princess Grace of Monaco. I kept that one purely because of her. She was so special, with this warmth and grace that really stood out.

The 1979 season wrapped up with the traditional Masters tournament, held in the middle of January. It was a kind of final showdown of the previous year's ATP Tour, with the top eight players battling it out. Like other tournaments, it started with a group stage, but here the competition was intense right from the start. You were facing the best of the best.

I made it through my group. In the semi-final, I beat McEnroe in a tough three-set match, and in the final, I faced Vitas, who had beaten Connors in his own semi. It was clear that all the major finals that year involved me and the big-name Americans.

I got my perfect end to a fantastic season, one of my best.

But even then, there was still a little nagging thought in the back of my mind. Something the medium had said during one of our talks at the house in Long Island. That I would never win the US Open. And that my relationship with Mariana might not last.

But we had just started planning our wedding.

15

Peak and Panic

When 1980 began, everything was at its peak. This was my prime, even if I didn't realise it at the time. The results that year would reflect my total focus and determination.

But somewhere around this time, and despite how well everything was going, I started to feel a creeping sense of panic. I never got any peace, had no private life. Any time we tried to go out to a restaurant, the international press was waiting outside, trying to snap photos. No meal in the world is good enough to make that bearable. The only time I got any real quiet was in my hotel room, and even that had started to feel more and more like a prison. I was let out to play my matches, expected to perform, then locked back in again. I was enjoying myself on the court, yet everything else around me felt like chaos.

On top of it all, there was a terrifying incident during one of the transatlantic flights. When you fly as much as I did, between tournaments in different parts of the world, it's no surprise that scary things happen from time to time. That day, I was flying from London to New York on Concorde, the supersonic plane that could get you from Europe to the US in just over three hours. Right as we lifted off, there was a sound like an explosion. A loud bang, and soon afterwards the captain announced over the speaker that one, or maybe several, tyres had burst on take-off and that we'd need to make an emergency landing. Panic broke out on board. Everyone was terrified, but the flight attendants still rolled out the drink carts. Today, safety procedures would probably be different, but back then it felt like no one believed we were going to make it, so nothing really mattered any more.

I don't exactly remember how I reacted, but I do know I didn't panic. It was out of my control, so I let it be. That's how I tend to approach things I can't influence. What happens, happens.

We circled over the English Channel for a long time to use up as much fuel as possible. Heathrow was in full emergency mode, ambulances and fire trucks everywhere, the runway coated in foam. While we were circling the Channel, people on board got more and more panicked, and very drunk. But we landed safely in the end. I don't remember exactly how, but there must've been a least a few functioning wheels since the pilot managed to taxi us to the gate.

A few hours later, I had to board another flight to continue the trip across the Atlantic. Most passengers chose to stay on the ground after what had happened, so when the next plane took off a little bit later it was only half full. But I didn't have a choice, I had to get to New York for the next tournament. Was this when the darker thoughts really started creeping in? Maybe. But I'd already been through a few close calls where, if I hadn't been lucky, I could've died. Maybe I had a guardian angel, like that time the car flipped. Someone looking out for me.

In my day, no one really talked about records, number of wins, or on what surfaces, not like they do now. These days, everything's tracked, from how many matches or tournaments someone wins in a row and on which surface, to how many aces and double faults they hit in a match. There are stats for everything now – a lot of it is thanks to the betting companies who want people to gamble on matches.

I won my first ATP title in Auckland in 1974. That was just six years earlier, and from there I kept getting better, winning more titles. In 1976, I won seven; in '77, twelve; and the year after, nine. My best year so far had been 1979, with thirteen ATP titles. Now I was out to beat my own record, and everything pointed to me succeeding.

The season started just as well as the year before. I won the Masters in New York, beating Vitas Gerulaitis in straight sets in the final. Right after the match, I went to Antigua with Ove Bengtson and his wife Lotta to relax and hang out, a trip I'd really been looking forward to. Unfortunately, almost as soon as the plane landed, I came down with a nasty fever. I spent an entire week in Antigua without even getting out of bed. But I was glad I'd managed to play the Masters and that I would recover in time for the next tournament. Not that I was much fun for Ove and Lotta as a travel companion.

Before the important clay court season began, something else big was on the agenda. Mariana and I had decided to get married that year, and now it was time for my bachelor party. I didn't really have time for it, but Vitas was the one organising everything. He planned it for March so it wouldn't interfere too much with my schedule. Vitas decided it was going to be in Florida, so we flew to Miami and Turnberry Isle, where a friend of his had built a resort we could stay at.

During the party weekend, we had two penthouses to

ourselves. It was quite the setup, Vitas had made sure it was a real party for everyone who came. As a welcome gift, everyone got a bathrobe with 'Björn Borg's Bachelor Party' printed on the back. My dad and grandfather were there, of course, and they took it upon themselves to act as bouncers. They checked the names of the invited girls, pretending there was a guest list, even though the page was completely blank. When people arrived at the party, they were totally thrown off. They were asked how long they planned to stay, what they wanted to eat and drink. No one had expected an interrogation. My grandfather didn't speak a word of English and my dad could barely make himself understood, and only when he wanted to. So it turned into this weird, hilarious interview in Swenglish that no one understood. But my dad and grandfather had a great time anyway joking around with the guests Vitas had invited.

I don't think anyone there thought that I was ready to get married – least of all me, and probably not Mariana either. My tennis friends especially didn't get why we were in such a rush. It wasn't like anyone was pressuring us, not her parents, not mine.

We really were good together, but even from the start, it felt like a tennis marriage. We met through tennis, and everything in our lives revolved around it. I didn't have to introduce her to anything or explain my lifestyle, she already knew what it took and what I had to do. She never made demands, and she fully embraced the role of my girlfriend, just there to support me. But things moved fast after that dinner in Paris and her trip with me to Wimbledon. What takes years for most couples happened in just a few months for us. We bonded quickly. We were the same age, but she ended up having to take care of me, almost like a mother figure, while I was off winning on the tennis court. It wasn't exactly fair, and I often felt guilty about it.

Anyway, the bachelor party was done, and there wasn't much

time for second thoughts. We had arrived in Florida a few days early and stayed a few days after to recover. We needed it after that weekend. I had an important season to focus on.

Back on the circuit, I was playing incredible tennis. At the end of March, right after the bachelor party, I played the Monte Carlo Open as usual, and didn't drop a single set. I beat Guillermo Vilas in the final. It was the perfect dress rehearsal for Paris, where I was the strong favourite to win my third straight title, and fifth overall.

My game was at its peak, and I was really looking forward to the coming weeks. I stepped onto the court for each match full of confidence, totally pumped to play. Leading up to the final in Paris, I barely lost any games. And there I faced my old friend Vitas Gerulaitis once again. By then, we'd played many matches, and I was probably his toughest opponent, even though we were such close friends. He never beat me, but he came close a few times, especially in what might've been our best match ever, at Wimbledon two years earlier.

This time I won easily in straight sets and got to lift the trophy again. As usual after a win in Paris, I celebrated with a great dinner at a good restaurant, had a glass of champagne, and then turned my attention towards Wimbledon.

16

Fire and Ice

'Time!'

The umpire's voice snapped me out of my reverie. 'Finally,' I thought. This was it. I was incredibly nervous, which actually wasn't like me. I usually felt a few nerves, sure, but never like this. If I managed to defend my title, it would be my fifth straight Wimbledon win, something no one else had done in the modern era. I'd make history.

This was the match everyone had been waiting for: the so-called dream final on Saturday, 5 July 1980, between me and the new world number two, John McEnroe. While I was out to win my fifth title, John had the chance to claim his first. It was our first time facing each other at Wimbledon, and the media had already dubbed it a legendary duel. The British press didn't hold back. They created such a frenzy it felt like the whole thing might explode. I was ranked number one, John number two, so it wasn't surprising we were meeting, but it was the match everyone had anticipated.

We were cast as total opposites and labelled 'Fire & Ice'. I was always portrayed as the typical Swede, quiet, cool, composed. John, on the other hand, had made a name for himself with his fiery outbursts and cocky New York attitude. A classic American who seemed to thrive on arguing and yelling on the court.

We were both in peak form after big tournament wins. In my case it was the French Open where I didn't lose a single set. The press couldn't get enough of the drama, and in the lead-up to the match, they had already written pages and pages about it. Of course, the British papers were especially invested and had declared it the greatest match ever played, before a single serve had even been hit.

Mariana and Labbe were the only ones with me at Wimbledon that year. My parents were at home. They always tried to attend when they could but didn't want to put any more pressure on me, trying to treat it like just another match. I'm sure they were far more nervous than they let on.

As usual, we stayed somewhere off the beaten path, the same hotel, the same suite as every year: the Holiday Inn in Hampstead. It let us keep to ourselves, unlike the other players who stayed in designated player hotels. As usual, I was super-stitious – nothing could be different from the previous year if things had gone well. Mariana always brought a lucky charm, often a stuffed animal. I always had to sit in the same chair on the court, so I would often jog onto Centre Court to grab it first. I never shaved during the tournament and only wore striped Fila shirts, preferably green. I always brought the exact same number of towels onto the court. We always rented the same type of car, it had to be a Saab. Labbe drove, just like he had since I was a junior. One year we were promised the same model, but just after we set off, Labbe said, 'We've got to turn

around. This isn't the right car.' Turned out the Saab didn't have
a radio, something we'd always had before. Labbe kept track of
everything.

At the Holiday Inn, we ordered room service and took it
easy. Total sexual abstinence. And we always ate the same
meal: meat, potatoes, vegetables and salad. With the amount
I trained, I needed all the calories I could get, so I also treated
myself to some ice cream afterwards. The fact is I love ice cream,
especially real Italian pistachio, and I can eat tons of it. I rarely
took supplements, but if I needed to, I'd top up with salt or iron
tablets. And I always ate lots of fruit.

Two days earlier, after my semi-final against Brian Gottfried,
I had walked off court, sweaty, satisfied, and most importantly,
with a huge sense of relief. I had handled the pressure, my own
and the world's, and made it to the final. The last obstacle was
out of the way, and I headed to the locker room to shower and
get ready. It was quiet and calm in there – most of the players
were already out, and it smelled better by the end of the tournament. Early on, it's chaos. Everyone fights for the same lockers
they had the year before. Once assigned, it's yours for the entire
event. These days, Wimbledon has been remodelled, you don't
have to cram into shared spaces any more. And thankfully,
there's no clay dust on the floor like in Paris.

When I was ready, it was time for the usual press conference
and TV interviews.

'How does it feel?'

That's probably the question I've been asked most in my life.
All I really wanted to say was, 'Good' and then leave. By now,
I knew I had to give longer answers, but talking was never my
thing. It was always a relief when it was over. I was still in my
bubble, but I could still enjoy the semi-final win a little. I'd lived

up to everyone's expectations, and my own. I was in yet another final, my fifth in a row.

Just a few hours earlier, John had done the same. In many ways, he represented the new wave of tennis. Yet I was only twenty-four, not exactly a tour veteran. Maybe it was the fact that I'd broken through so young that I was considered 'experienced', especially compared to John. Game-wise, I had a slight advantage. We'd met seven times before, I'd won four. I'd only dropped two sets in the whole tournament, and physically, I felt great. I was peaking, and it was time to refocus for the final.

The day before the final started like always, with breakfast in the hotel room. Then I trained from ten to noon at the Cumberland tennis club nearby. I would've preferred to hit with Vitas as usual, but this time I needed a lefty to get a feel for John's angles. He was a master of the unexpected. We chose Ray Ruffels from Australia, and in hindsight it's easy to say that he did a great job.

After lunch at the club, we tried to head back to the hotel, but about fifty journalists were waiting outside in a crowd. Everyone was hoping for a good photo, or ideally, an interview. The club had our backs, as always. They made sure we felt calm and safe. No journalist was allowed through, and we made it to the car. It was, after all, a private tennis and cricket club with exclusive membership.

The same thing happened when we arrived at the hotel – photographers everywhere. But we managed to slip past and get up to the room, where we watched Evonne Goolagong Cawley beat Chris Evert Lloyd in the women's final. The only question that remained was who would be her dance partner at the traditional final ball.

Later that evening, we played cards, but I got quieter and more tense. I felt incredibly stressed inside, though I didn't show it. Anyone who didn't know me would never have noticed, but Labbe and Mariana could tell. They fell silent with me.

I've always needed a lot of sleep, so after a simple room-service dinner, I went to bed early. I wanted to be asleep before ten, in a cool, dark room. Total darkness, no distractions. Later in life, I've had to compromise on that since Patricia likes to sleep with the curtains open. These days it's not a big deal, but during my tennis career, it was non-negotiable.

I wouldn't say I slept well that night, but at least I stayed in bed.

On the day of the final, I woke up early, before the others. Right away, my thoughts started racing, and there was no chance of falling back asleep. I tried thinking about anything other than the final, but it was useless. I knew there'd be a long wait ahead, the match wouldn't even start until the afternoon.

These days, people talk a lot about visualising, seeing yourself win, picturing yourself lifting the trophy. That wasn't something I ever used. Instead, I tried to think of something else entirely. My mind wandered to the distinctive grass on Centre Court at Wimbledon.

There's something about how we Swedes feel about lawns and grassy fields. Is there anything better than waking up on an early summer morning and walking barefoot through dewy grass? The sun slowly warming the ground until steam starts to rise. I knew that the court on Centre Court was badly worn down along the baseline and in other spots where the sun had taken a toll on the grass over the course of the tournament. The day after the final, the court would be closed so it could be restored for the next year. Apparently, they even let a hawk loose over the grounds each morning to scare off pigeons that might disrupt play or damage the courts. But I didn't know that at the time.

Mariana started stirring in bed, and I could hear Labbe moving around in the shared lounge between our adjoining suites. I've never been one to lie around in the mornings and, especially on a day like this, my entire body felt restless. It was time to get up and face the task ahead. 'One day to go, one more match to win', I told myself.

As usual, we ordered breakfast to the room. We sat together in the shared area and had a proper, hearty breakfast, more like a lunch. If I'd been quiet the night before, it was nothing compared to how I was that morning. I barely looked up, completely inside my bubble. The truth was, I just wanted to get out there and play. Waiting only made things worse. The stress and nerves kept building.

I didn't know if John felt the same way. He usually slept well, and there had even been times at smaller tournaments when someone had to wake him up so he wouldn't miss his match. That was the complete opposite of me, but honestly, it sounded kind of nice.

We drove to the Cumberland club again to hit with Ray Ruffels. Normally, you'd warm up on a practice court at the venue itself, but I didn't want to set foot at Wimbledon until it was time to walk onto Centre Court. Labbe had arranged for us to hit for forty-five minutes at Cumberland instead. The drive over felt like an out-of-body experience: I could see that we were moving, but it was like everything was frozen still.

As soon as we arrived, I stripped off my warm-ups and stepped straight onto the court. Things got easier immediately. I didn't have to think any more, my body took over, and I could feel myself relaxing. I had sawdust in my pockets as usual. It was my way of keeping my palms dry and keeping a tighter grip on the racket, and there were always traces of it on the court after I played.

The warm-up went well. We ordered the same lunch as always. The club had even arranged a private room where I could lie down and rest a bit before the match. It saved me the trip back to the hotel and helped me conserve energy. Eventually, it was time to head to the stadium. The drive from Hampstead to Wimbledon was long, and that Saturday it felt endless. No one said a word. Not even the car stereo was on, just the muffled sounds of traffic filling the silence.

Everything changed as we neared the arena. There were huge crowds gathered outside. So many people were there, all waiting to see me and John in the final.

When I went into the big locker room, I noticed that John was already there. Maybe he too hadn't been able to sleep as well as usual? He was usually never the first one there and had probably warmed up at Wimbledon and not at Cumberland like I had.

It was just the two of us now, and the tension in the room was so thick you could feel it in the air. The mind games had already started. We changed side by side, stealing glances at each other in silence. Sure, we'd been in this kind of situation before, but never on this stage, and never with so much at stake for both of us. Finally, we got the signal. We stood up and headed towards the court. The wait was over.

When we stepped onto Centre Court at ten past two on that Saturday afternoon, the crowd erupted. You could feel the excitement, they were already in a frenzy and shouted out in joy. The British audience didn't exactly love John. They thought he was a spoiled 'superbrat' from New York. But people sometimes forget the pressure he was under too, especially from his family, who had invested everything in his career and his path to becoming number one. There was talk early on that this pressure was behind many of his outbursts, that he struggled to cope with it. These days, he's totally different and at peace with himself. It's as if today there's a calm about my dear friend.

But back then, both of us were feeling the weight of enormous expectations. Anything could happen that afternoon, and the only certainty was that something would.

We walked onto the court at the same time, but as usual, I rushed to get to my chair first. Honestly, I didn't have to, everyone knew my habits by then, and the other players knew how I was and always let me have the chair I wanted. Despite the massive crowd, I could clearly see from my seat what was happening in the stands. I saw Mariana and Labbe in their spots and recognised where a few of my friends were sitting. But that was just a fraction of the audience. Outside the stadium, there were people who couldn't get tickets, or couldn't afford them. Around the world, millions of people were watching on TV or listening on the radio.

One of them, that very Saturday, was Nelson Mandela, the South African freedom fighter imprisoned on Robben Island off Cape Town. Even in captivity, he was allowed a small transistor radio, and at that moment, he forgot he was in prison, because in his mind, he was right there in London. How do I know that? Years later, John and I were invited to lunch at his home in Johannesburg. We were there for a senior tour event, and he had heard about it. He wanted to thank us personally for that unforgettable match in 1980. He was every bit as kind and warm as you'd imagine. It was incredibly powerful to meet him and sit at his table.

Back on Centre Court, we were introduced, and then it was time to flip a coin to decide who would serve first. I was quick to take off my warm-ups, while John took his time – I'm an efficient person and like to get things done quickly. The toss was done the usual way, heads or tails, and whenever I won, I always chose to receive first.

Then we had a few minutes for our warm-up, testing all our shots: backhand, forehand, volley, and smash. We were introduced to the crowd, and the cheers grew louder. After a few serves on each side, the umpire called out: 'Time!'

I lost the first set quickly, 6–1. During the changeover, I sat down to calm myself, take a deep breath and get my head back into the game. There's no one to help you make decisions out there. You're completely alone with your thoughts. I knew how I needed to play, and that I had to be at my absolute best to win. I got ready to come out strong in the second set.

But things didn't go much better once we started up again. I was still on the back foot. John ended up with a set point, which I somehow saved. I turned the set in my favour and went on to win it 7–5.

It was absolutely critical for me to take home that set, and after that, I was able to play more freely. Everything just flowed – John noticed it, too – and the match swung in my favour. I took the third set 6–3, and now I had the psychological edge.

Fourth set. It was closer now, but I was still in control. Suddenly I was up 5–4, and at 40–15 I had two championship points. I was so close, my fifth straight Wimbledon title was within reach. I served what I thought was an ace. The crowd erupted, everyone thought it was over.

But the umpire called it out. Even today, I still wonder if that ball wasn't actually in. But I stayed calm and walked back to the baseline to continue. I hit a good second serve and followed it up by rushing the net, but John passed me.

One match point left. I served again and came to the net, but John hit a perfect return. Deuce. Next point, I hit the net. Advantage John. Then he hit a laser-sharp return on the next serve that I didn't even have a chance to reach. The game was his. 5–5. We each held our next service games easily, and suddenly we were in a tiebreak.

To say it was long would be an understatement. When the score hit 11–11, the BBC commentator said the now-famous line: 'Nothing more can happen. Everything has happened.' But the match continued with the same level of drama. I managed to both earn and lose all five match points in that tiebreak. After twenty-two minutes, John won the tiebreak 18–16.

It was now 2–2 and the match had turned again. We were both playing the best tennis of our lives, and that tiebreak has since gone down as one of the greatest moments in sports history. People still ask me about it. Everyone who watched has their own memory of that fourth set.

I walked back to my chair with heavy steps. During the break before the fifth and final set, I had already lost the match in my mind. I sat there wondering what had gone wrong. John, meanwhile, was fired up, like the young rebel he was. His swagger was back, and you could see the confidence in every movement. He was full of energy, charging back onto the court.

And then something surprising happened: the crowd switched. For the first time, the Wimbledon audience fell in love with John. He had been playing spectacularly, the kind of game he'd always been capable of, but which had been overshadowed by his temper and tendency to argue with every decision. He respected me, and we were both playing incredible tennis.

The fifth set began, and I struggled at first. John had a chance to break my serve right away. Somehow, I held on and won the game, which turned out to be hugely important. Getting a good start in any set is crucial, but especially in the fifth. That hold calmed my body down and I could breathe a bit easier. The tiebreak had taken so much out of me, and I was still frustrated over losing it. If John had broken me in that opening game, it might've been too much to come back from. I won my next serves more easily, though the set overall was even.

At 7–6, it was John's turn to serve again. When we stood up from our chairs, I had the mental edge. He had to hold serve just to stay in the match.

I ended up playing a great return game and ramped up the pressure on him. My returns were landing deep, and soon I had two more match points, on his serve this time. I only needed one of them to finally end it. Still, I'd already missed seven.

The crowd was roaring, but like always I just blew into my hand for grip and focused. John served and rushed the net. I couldn't pass him right away with my return, but his volley wasn't clean, and I sent a backhand past him.

Victory!

I dropped to my knees and clasped my hands together, as if thanking the heavens. I could hardly believe it was real. I stumbled to my feet and walked over to shake John's hand. Then I thanked the umpire and sank into my chair. The whole crowd was going wild, but I was completely drained, utterly exhausted, every ounce of strength gone from my body. My mind was blank, completely wiped out by the mental exertion. I didn't even look up at Mariana or Labbe in the stands. Was I happy? I don't know. I was entirely gone. But the match replayed itself in my head as I stared straight ahead, eyes unfocused. 'Unbelievable,' I whispered to myself. 'I actually won. Unbelievable.'

I remember many of my matches only in fragments. This isn't one of them. The flow of this match is still crystal clear in my mind, even though the memories are both razor-sharp and blurry at the same time. Probably because I'd never been so intensely focused, for such a long period, as I was that day. I could refresh my memory completely by just watching the match because it's available, but I've never done so. Not that one, and not any other match either. What's done is done.

Nowadays, when John and I meet, we don't talk about our old battles. I guess we're similar that way – we both look forward, not back. Together, we wrote tennis history, but it wasn't something we thought about then, and it's not something we dwell on now. Sure, I could feel proud, but that wasn't how I thought when I was on the court. When I played, I was completely locked into myself. I usually knew what mistakes I made, but it didn't help to dwell on them. I might've made the wrong call at times, but I stuck to my game, and it worked. John once said the hardest thing about facing me was that I was impossible to read. When others got tired, I just kept going, like a wind-up robot. I wore people down. Sooner or later, the moment came when I gained the upper hand.

No one, not even me at my absolute best, can play a flawless match, especially not one that goes five sets. But every match has that one turning point, and I was often the one who seized it. That's probably what made me number one in the world: I could win the most important points.

The trophy ceremony began, and all I waited to hear in the roar of the crowd was: 'And the winner is . . .'

I walked up to the trophy with the lightest steps of my life. It felt just like when I was a kid, running down to Badparken in Södertälje to play tennis. I lifted the trophy effortlessly, and as always at Wimbledon, I kissed it. That had become my thing.

After the ceremony, I returned to the locker room. John was already there, but now they'd also let in some VIP guests who wanted to congratulate me. We looked at each other, and just like before the match, we exchanged only a glance, no words.

Further inside the locker area, past the massage tables and supply rooms, there was a bathroom with a tub. I literally locked myself in, turned the lock carefully, and finally had a moment to myself. No one would come near me there. I filled the tub and slowly sank into the water. I honestly don't know what I was thinking. It was completely silent, but at the same time, my mind was full of thoughts. I don't know how long I stayed there, probably half an hour. My fingers looked like raisins by the time I got out, and I'd recovered just enough to stand up and walk around.

That's when it started to sink in. I had actually won Wimbledon five times in a row. There was going to be a ton of attention at the press conference, and I knew I needed to save some energy for that, and for the TV interviews afterwards. Of course, it's always easier when you've won. There's nothing worse than losing a match and being forced to answer the same tired old question:

'How does it feel?'

Like hell. That's the only honest answer you want to give. I would never blame my loss on mistakes or shortcomings. If I lost, it's always because my opponent played better, and he deserves credit for that. There are no excuses. That's just how I am.

I gathered myself for what was waiting outside that door and stepped out to face the press. And this time, the answer to 'How does it feel?' came a little easier:

'Good. Really good.'

17

The Circus After Wimbledon

The historic Wimbledon victory was in the bag, but there was still one more thing to get through: the final night's ball, where the men's singles champion traditionally dances with the women's winner.

If I found it awkward answering journalists' questions, this was even worse. The dance hadn't got any easier, even though it was my fifth time doing it. Nothing against the women's champ, Evonne Goolagong Cawley – we both did our best to make it through the dance – but honestly, all I wanted was to sneak away and enjoy my own victory dinner. Eat and drink well with my closest people, maybe hit a nightclub and celebrate properly.

Labbe was always there to celebrate, of course, he went full throttle every time. When my parents were in town, they naturally came along to the afterparties too. Everyone wanted to celebrate a win, and those celebrations often lasted all night. That's just how tennis is, you bring your family along, and no one thinks anything of it. To succeed in tennis, you need your family's support.

As soon as the first dance and the formal part of the evening were over, Labbe, Mariana and I finally managed to slip out of the ball and head elsewhere. We ended up at the hottest place in 1980, a private club called Tramp, which is still around today. Like all private clubs, it had a distinct sense of glamour and exclusivity, and just getting let into that dimly lit room felt like something special. You could run into all sorts of celebrities there, and I enjoyed every second of it.

After two of my previous Wimbledon wins, we'd also had dinner at Tramp, both times with movie legend Ingrid Bergman at the table. And just like those years, this year's host was Erik Steiner, the 'Poker King', as Labbe always insisted on calling him. Erik was a good friend of mine and of my parents, and he'd watched the final this year from the stands alongside Mariana and Labbe. He was a well-known poker player and owned several casinos in London. Erik knew Ingrid Bergman's husband Lars Schmidt, and I guess they found the Swedish connection amusing. For me, it was a big deal. She was someone who preferred to stay out of the spotlight. That was something we had in common.

I've heard that the movie *The Cincinnati Kid* with Steve McQueen is based on Erik Steiner's life. I don't know if that's true, but Erik was such a larger-than-life character that I wouldn't be surprised. He was based mostly in London, but he also had a beautiful house in Marbella, 'Casa Bananas', where my parents would sometimes visit. Erik was one of the few real friends our family had during those years. A lot of people came and went, probably more interested in being seen than in actually being there. Erik was genuine.

One of the times when my parents were visiting him in

Spain, they rented a car at Málaga airport. When they arrived at Casa Bananas, Erik told them to just leave the luggage in the car, his staff would handle both the bags and the car. As usual, he welcomed them with champagne in the garden on the other side of the house, and time flew by. When it was finally time to change clothes, the luggage had indeed been taken care of and brought up to their room, but someone had forgotten to shut the car doors. That turned into a problem, because Erik's German Shepherds, who were always running loose around the yard, had turned the rental car into their own little party zone. They'd chewed up the upholstery and whatever else was loose inside. The rental company staff were completely stunned when they caught sight of the wreck once it was returned, and my parents were embarrassed, but they'd had a great time.

This year's dinner at Tramp was a hit, thanks largely to Erik. It was an intimate, private dinner with about ten of us, all invited by him. Physically, the trophy stayed at Wimbledon, but it was etched in my mind for ever. Of course, we didn't get much sleep that night, and the next day, Mariana and I were already boarding a flight to Bucharest. I'd skipped Båstad that year for something more important.

It was time to start seriously preparing for the wedding.

Life was good. Money was flowing in, my tennis career couldn't have been better, and now I was getting married. For better or worse, I was now a household name in most of the world, so the wedding was closely followed by the press. It had only been a few weeks since the dramatic Wimbledon final, so the wedding felt like a kind of romantic sequel to the fairy tale.

We'd chosen Bucharest for the wedding, with an Orthodox ceremony set for 24 July. Despite the media's interest, we managed to keep it fairly private, with only a small group of guests. The only one of my tennis friends there was Ilie Năstase, probably because he was Romanian. I don't know why the others didn't come; maybe the distance put them off, or maybe they just wanted to stay home. Travelling and staying in hotels is all you ever do as a tennis player.

Now we were officially husband and wife. When we stepped out of the church, a line of kids from the Romanian Tennis Federation stood holding up their rackets to form an arch, and we walked through a tunnel of tennis rackets. The very next day, we flew back to Monaco and held a wedding reception at the Monte Carlo Country Club, my training base. It was important to celebrate there, since the club had always supported me through my career. Among the guests were Princess Grace and Prince Albert. We stayed a few more days before continuing our little 'wedding tour' to Marbella on the southern coast of Spain, at the resort Puente Romano. There we held a second reception, and 'everyone' was there. Easily over a hundred journalists and photographers swarmed around us, all fighting to get the best shot. It was completely insane.

The wedding itself was beautiful and well planned, but with the two receptions afterwards, there wasn't any time left for a honeymoon. Instead, it was time to focus on the next big tournament: the US Open.

Mariana and I headed straight to Long Island to set up base camp. I kicked things off by playing the Canadian Open in Toronto, a key warm-up tournament for the US Open. It's kind of like Queen's is for Wimbledon, or Monte Carlo and Rome are for Paris. But something troubling happened in the final against Ivan Lendl: I felt a sudden pain in one knee.

'Not again,' I thought. Something always seemed to go wrong

before the US Open, some irritation or weird injury that came out of nowhere. Labbe saw right away that something was off and signalled to me to stop the match, which I did. It wasn't worth the risk.

Back on Long Island, I got treatment so my knee could heal in time for the US Open, and luckily, it did. Mariana and I were able to continue our carefree life as newlyweds.

Despite the knee scare and all the media noise around the tournament, I was completely focused on finally getting my revenge at the US Open. That year, 1980, was supposed to be my year, I was the best in the world. But what can I say? Instead, it turned out to be one of my toughest losses.

I made it to the final, as expected, where I once again faced a truly revenge-hungry John McEnroe. It was another long, tight, well-played five-set battle, but this time, he came out on top. John had got his revenge for Wimbledon, and I was devastated, so much so that I still don't really like to think or talk about that match, even today.

If I had to rank my losses, that US Open final hurt the most, right up there with my loss to Connors at the same tournament in 1976. I probably had my best shots at winning the tournament during those years, if only a few more things had gone my way. But I guess you could say that as much bad luck as I had at the US Open, I had just as much good fortune at Wimbledon.

No matter how I look at it, Wimbledon was always the biggest tournament for me. I would never trade one of my five titles there for a single US Open win. There was something special about walking onto Centre Court at Wimbledon, it felt like home. Every player wants to win a Grand Slam, of course. But Americans dream of the US Open, Spaniards and South Americans want to play in the Stade Roland Garros at the French Open, Aussies want to be in Melbourne for the Australian Open. For me, Wimbledon was everything.

Somehow, life moved on after the 1980 US Open. Mariana and I stayed in New York a while longer and relaxed at the house on Long Island. We had a fun time with friends, which helped soften the blow a little.

Later that autumn, Vitas and I decided to play a series of exhibition matches in South America, what was called the South American Tour, hitting countries like Venezuela, Brazil, Paraguay, Chile, Peru and Argentina. It was a bit of a circus. Every time we arrived in a new country, it felt like a mini state visit, with meetings with presidents and grand building tours.

We started in Caracas, and everything went smoothly. Then we were due to fly to São Paulo. Flights were usually at night, and when Labbe, Vitas and I arrived at the airport late in the evening, we suddenly found out that our booking had been lost. It was hard to understand how they'd managed to 'lose' a reservation, especially because it was for first-class tickets. A fellow traveller let it slip that they'd probably just sold our seats to someone willing to pay more.

All we could do was watch our plane take off without us. We also knew that 10,000 tickets had already been sold for our exhibition in São Paulo, and now there was no way to get there in time.

Or so we thought, until someone tipped us off to try a military airport and charter a plane ourselves. We had no idea where that airport was, but we took a chance, jumped into a taxi, and told the driver to take us to any airfield with planes. After a wild ride – we had no clue where we even were – we finally pulled up somewhere. We looked at each other and quietly wondered if the driver was joking because it looked more like a graveyard for antique aircraft than an actual airstrip. The cab took off, but we managed to find someone who said they could help us. There was only one problem: their best plane wasn't available right then. So we chose a plane that still looked intact and as it was being towed out of the hangar, we said a prayer that this wouldn't turn out to be a terrible decision.

The moment we got airborne, the whole plane shook violently, but we started to think we might actually make it in one piece. Then we realised there was no heat and no air conditioning. The cabin got so cold we risked frostbite. We put on every piece of clothing we had, huddled together and toughed it out, shivering through the flight.

When we landed in São Paulo there was no time to spare. We headed straight to the arena. We changed clothes in the back of the taxi and arrived just in time, where the frantic organisers were waiting for us. The match was about to start. It went quickly, but if I thought that plane story was going to be the only odd part of the trip, I was wrong.

We had a few hours at a nice hotel, finally a real bed, but the next day we were off to Asunción, Paraguay. We were exhausted when we arrived and were met by a host family we'd be staying with. That evening, I played Paraguay's national hero, Victor Pecci, and I was already wiped out before we even got started. I lost three sets to nil, and the whole arena exploded in celebration. When I got back to the house, I collapsed onto the couch. Vitas, however, was never too tired. He picked up a guitar and played for the host family, apparently giving them a night they'd never forget. I don't remember any of it, I was asleep before he hit the first chord.

After a few hours of sleep, it was time to head to Lima, Peru, where I played Vitas in a fun, high-energy match. We always brought out the best in each other, and the crowd was into it, the atmosphere was great. Afterwards, Vitas didn't want to head back to the hotel just yet, so he started asking around for the best club in town. After some very sketchy directions, we ended up in front of a garage door, which you had to lift like a warehouse shutter to get inside. Sure enough, it was packed, a full-on party, and Vitas was thrilled.

We stayed out later than we'd planned, and with just a few hours of sleep, we were off to Santiago, Chile. Tickets had sold out so quickly that they'd added an extra match day. By that point, I'll admit, the level of tennis had dropped quite a bit. Labbe tried his best to keep us going, but we were completely drained after all the travel and sleep deprivation. He even grumbled about the insanity of playing so many matches that 'don't count' beyond the money rolling into the bank. And sure, he had a point. But even if the tennis wasn't always top-notch, everyone was having a great time, players and spectators alike. It felt like a festival everywhere we went those weeks.

After Chile, Vitas headed back to New York, while I continued with Labbe to the Mar del Plata Invitational in Argentina. I was matched up against national icon and hometown hero Guillermo Vilas. I knew I needed rest if I was going to stand a chance, and thanks to an extra day in Mar del Plata I finally got a full night's sleep and didn't wake up until noon the next day.

In Argentina, everything happens late. The tennis event was held at a massive stadium where the local football team usually played. It was completely packed, the entire arena buzzing with anticipation. I was finally well-rested for the first time in ages, and as Labbe always said, that's the key to winning. I ended up playing surprisingly well and actually blew Vilas off the court. The crowd wasn't too happy about it. Vilas had taken it seriously, he'd even done a training camp before the match. The crowd may have been disappointed, but Vilas's coach, Ion Țiriac, was even more upset. And the fact that the scoreline had been so one-sided only made it worse.

After the match, we travelled to Buenos Aires, where we'd catch our flight home the next morning. But we still had hours to kill, so we tracked down a club everyone said was 'the place to be'. We showed up at 2 a.m., only to be greeted by a woman vacuuming the carpet. I asked if they were closed.

'No, no,' she said. 'We haven't opened yet.'

That's when we gave up. We were done with nightclubs for that trip, and probably for the best. It was time to head to the airport.

Back in Europe, we flew straight to Copenhagen, where the next exhibition event was waiting. I had two hours between landing and when I was scheduled to play my first match. It was a four-player event: me, Adriano Panatta, Jimmy Connors and Vitas Gerulaitis, who was now well-rested after his time off on Long Island. I faced Connors, but I didn't have much left to give.

That was the final match in the exhibition contract I had signed. And I had to admit, Labbe was right. It probably hadn't been the best idea. At least, not performance-wise. But in every other way, it had been a few weeks full of incredible experiences, especially with Labbe by my side. Sometimes, you've got to just have some fun too.

18

'Leave Me Alone'

By New Year 1981, just about everything in my life looked perfect. I was ready for a new season and had taken time to recharge. But this would be the year everything started to change. I just didn't know it yet.

As the year began, I played the Masters, the tournament that closed out the 1980 ATP tour. Back then, the Masters was always held at Madison Square Garden in New York, and this was the first year they made the final the best of five sets. I won the tournament again, just like the year before, this time facing Ivan Lendl in the final.

As usual, I took a long break at the start of the year to focus on training, before ramping up the matches in the spring. I kept doing what I was supposed to and played some fantastic tennis. Spring came and went, Paris was approaching, but somewhere around then, things began to shift. For the first time, I felt like tennis wasn't fun any more.

The motivation wasn't there like before, and I started turning

down some tournaments. And for the first time in my life, I also
didn't enjoy training the way I used to. Where I'd once trained
four hours a day outdoors, now it was one, maybe two. It felt
like it didn't matter, I was still beating everyone anyway. My
stubbornness kept me grinding, even if things didn't feel as fun.
I had always controlled my own training, Labbe never decided
for me, but it was starting to take a toll mentally. The best part
of my day was getting back to the hotel and shutting the door
behind me. And even that was weighing heavy on me, because
I knew I'd have to do it all over again the next day. I didn't have
a life any more. That's how it felt.

Another thing that bothered me was the total lack of security
at tournaments. Anyone could get to me. Journalists were all
over me from morning to night. It was a constant game of cat
and mouse, of locking myself in the hotel after matches, only
to face the same routine the next day. More and more, I found
myself thinking about life beyond tennis, everything I was
missing out on. Even just sitting at a restaurant, trying to eat in
peace, people would come up to me non-stop.

Looking back, that might've been the hardest part, not ever
being left alone. The only time I felt untouchable was on the
court. That had always been enough, but now, it wasn't any
more. The question that kept echoing inside me was: 'Is this
really what I'm supposed to do every day for the rest of my life?'

Each morning, I woke up with a growing sense of dread. I
started having panic attacks, a kind of claustrophobic feeling,
like I was trapped in a small, airless room.

Even my life as a newlywed with Mariana wasn't what it
seemed. It felt like our relationship was already running on
fumes. The world saw a romantic tennis fairytale wedding, but
deep down, I had already started to realise I might be done with
tennis soon. And that raised doubts about us too. Was Mariana

the person I'd spend the rest of my life with? We hadn't even talked about having kids. It felt like we both knew the marriage would work as long as I kept playing, but maybe not afterwards.

The win at the French Open turned out to be my last big title in tennis. By the time I arrived, I hadn't trained nearly as much as before, and that really upset Labbe. But he didn't have a say any more. I still listened to him, of course, but I was calling the shots. He could tell I had lost motivation, and it frustrated him no end.

Still, I had a level of play most others could only dream of. I faced Ivan Lendl again in this final, and even though I always wanted to win, my mind started messing with me. 'You're actually in a Grand Slam final,' I had to force myself to remember. It was harder to focus on every point. In the fifth set, I finally got fed up with myself. I wasn't going to lose this match. And I didn't.

But the thoughts of quitting kept pressing in. Perhaps it was strange, considering it wasn't a bad year. I had won the Masters and the French Open for a sixth time, a record that stood until Rafael Nadal broke it many years later. But I no longer knew exactly what I was looking for. I knew I was having more fun training at the SALK Hall with Peter Lundgren than I was playing Grand Slam finals. People thought we were nuts. Our practice sessions could go on for hours. People would come and go. 'You're still playing?' they'd ask when they came back.

When we went to London to prepare for Wimbledon, Labbe was sure I could win again, but I was struggling to motivate myself. These days, the competition is tougher and the prize money much higher, so I understand the pressure players feel walking onto a court. When I was playing, there wasn't as much money involved. Sure, every won match added up in the bank, but it was never just about money. Actually it's only a small part of it all. I had to want to win for other reasons, too. And I had lost that feeling.

Now I was back at Wimbledon in 1981 to defend my title. I had the chance to make history with a sixth straight win. And once again, the final was a rematch against my now constant rival: John McEnroe. Only this time, John played great tennis, and he won. I lost in four sets.

I had a set point to go up two sets to nil. If I'd taken it, who knows? The whole match might've gone differently. Between one set all and two-nil there's a huge mental difference. The whole time, I felt like I could win – more so than the year before, even. But I just didn't have it in me. My head wasn't in the right place.

My winning streak at Wimbledon was over. I stopped at forty-one straight victories in the tournament. That match was also the last Wimbledon final ever played with wooden rackets, a symbol of the big shift that was coming in tennis. New models and materials were taking over.

I had just lost a Wimbledon final. Normally, I would've been so furious that no one could talk to me for hours. But I didn't feel that way any more. The deep disappointment wasn't there. I had just blown the chance to win Wimbledon for the sixth time. Instead, I just thanked John for the match. 'This isn't me,' I remember thinking, sitting in my chair and watching John celebrate.

With his Wimbledon win, John McEnroe had taken over as world number one, but I was still ranked second. I remember seeing a stat once that said we were completely even going into that final set at Wimbledon, twenty sets all in our head-to-head matches. If that's true, we were basically inseparable. Then came

Sunday, 13 September 1981, John's third straight US Open title. Once again, he beat me in the final.

And here's the thing: I had received a death threat before my semi-final against Jimmy Connors. Actually, it was the second one during the same tournament. The threats came in early on, likely from someone who wanted an American in the top spot. The message was clear: if I stepped on court, I'd be killed. Naturally, it created a horrible sense of unease going out there. I was surrounded by bodyguards, but the arena at Flushing Meadows is huge. If someone really wanted to do something, it wouldn't have been that hard. When the match was finally over, no one from the tournament questioned why I left immediately. Maybe they were even relieved nothing had happened.

After losing to John in the final, I did the same thing I had after Wimbledon: I thanked him for the match and left for home. Straight to Long Island. No interview. No press conference. Nothing. You just don't do that, not then, not now. I don't think any other tennis player has ever done that.

We got in the car, Labbe, Mariana and I, and drove back home. When we arrived at the house on Long Island, it was already packed. Easily 100–150 people, friends and family, had gathered to be there if, or rather *when*, I won. Everyone had been waiting to celebrate a victory that never came. The moment I walked into the house, I could feel the disappointment sink into the room. It was awful. And no one was more disappointed than me. I left the house, walked straight down to the pool in the backyard, and grabbed a crate of beer.

'Leave me alone,' was all I said to anyone who asked. No one dared follow me, not even those closest to me. They knew what kind of state I was in. They could see it in my eyes: I needed to be alone.

*

I don't know how long I stayed there in the pool. I could hear the party going on inside the house. It was late, it was dark, but the house was lit up and full of noise. Laughter, chatter, the clinking of glasses. And all I could think was, I didn't belong in this world any more. Not in this house, not in a city like New York. What was I even doing here? I was just a regular guy from Södertälje. Now here I was, floating in a pool on Long Island in some luxury mansion, surrounded by people who all wanted something from me. All I could think was how miserable my life had become. The thoughts grew heavier by the second, and suddenly, everything felt ice-cold and crushing. What if I had won the match? Just another victory, then what?

That night, in the pool, I made up my mind. I was done. I was going to quit tennis. The thought had been creeping in since Wimbledon. But now I knew, there was absolutely no joy left in it for me. At the same time, I felt like I was nothing outside the tennis court. Everyone wanted a piece of me. I had already won almost everything, many times over. All good things must come to an end, I thought.

After lying there for hours, I eventually decided to go back into the party. I put on a smile, because I knew what was expected of me.

I knew how to play the game.

PART FOUR

Guardian Angel (1981–2000)

19

When It's Over, It's Over

How can you quit tennis before even turning twenty-six? That's what the whole world was asking. But the people closest to me weren't all that surprised. I'm not hard to read, and my lack of motivation had probably been obvious to Labbe, my parents and Mariana for some time.

It had nothing to do with John beating me. I had just had a season most players could only dream of – wins at the Masters, the French Open, Stuttgart, and runner-up finishes at both Wimbledon and the US Open. I was ranked number two in the world.

But I had been on top for a long time and needed new challenges. I'd held the world number one spot for 109 consecutive weeks. Not that I kept track at the time – I only found out later when a perfume was being launched in my name. It was called '109' and I probably looked confused when I heard the name. The team behind it said, 'You didn't know?' But I honestly had no idea, which says a lot, I guess.

I withdrew more and more, until I didn't even want to leave the house. That feeling of isolation just grew inside me, even though I had my family and Mariana nearby. She knew I wasn't happy with how my life was going, but not many others suspected. I was miserable no matter where I was, in Monte Carlo or in New York. That in itself became a problem.

'Where do I belong? Where's home, really?' These were questions I was asking myself all the time. All those years of constantly moving and living out of suitcases had left me completely rootless.

But I'd always loved Sweden, and now I longed to return. Contrary to what people thought, or even accused me of, I wasn't 'un-Swedish'. Quite the opposite. I was the definition of Swedishness, as those who really knew me understood. The move to Monaco was purely a business decision. It had nothing to do with how I felt about Sweden. When I was on tour, the hotel room was my home. In between tournaments, home was wherever my parents were staying. That meant I had no personal retreat, no place filled with memories or furniture I could call my own. With the same determination I had on court, I now knew I needed to get away from tennis and build a completely different life.

In hindsight, I can see that it was the wrong decision, because things actually ended up even worse. At first, right after I quit, it felt a bit like a long-awaited vacation. I could finally do whatever I wanted, no rigid schedules, no daily training, no total control over every minute of my life. I had earned a lot of prize money, especially towards the end of my career. And my sponsorship deals paid well too, so there was no financial pressure.

Outwardly, I told people I was just taking a break. That I needed some time off. But it was just for show. I had to maintain appearances, for sponsors, for everyone else. In my head, I had already quit, but the situation would be a sensitive one, so I couldn't go public with it yet. There are too many contracts in place when you're a tennis player. You can't just tell the truth. Everything would be affected. So I chose to say that I was just taking time off.

Despite the relief of finally having freedom, those feelings of loneliness and rootlessness stuck around. And my way of dealing with them was to self-medicate, with all kinds of things. It turned into a dangerous mix of drugs, pills and alcohol.

There were still a few tournaments I had promised to play, and I couldn't just blow them all off. In Geneva, they begged me to come, and I eventually did. It was an ATP event about a week after the US Open in September 1981. I actually played Mats Wilander in the first round – it was both our first and last match against each other. I played well, even if my head was spinning.

They had to drag me out of nightclubs every night, I just didn't want to go home. I was sick of everything. The later I could stay out, the better. A man named Bertrand Gros was often the one making sure I got back safely. 'Björn, you've got a match tomorrow, come on now,' he'd say, before physically escorting me back to the hotel and putting me to bed. 'Please, just one more hour,' was my usual response, but it fell on deaf ears.

Bertrand was Swiss and worked as a lawyer at IMG at the time. Later, he became chairman of Rolex. Our paths have crossed many times since then. But back then, when all I wanted to do was forget everything and keep partying, he made sure I got home each night. He cared, and he worried about me.

The tournament in Geneva ended up being my last win. I still played great tennis, no one beat me. Sometimes it works that way. When you stop caring, your body relaxes, just like when you're about to lose. I didn't care one bit if I won or lost.

Mariana and I were having bigger and bigger problems. She wasn't travelling with me as much any more, so she had no say in my increasingly wild nightlife. She lived her own life alongside my tennis, spending time with her parents, playing tennis, or going on her own trips.

When I officially announced, in early 1983, that I was retiring from tennis, that was also the official end of our marriage. She had been so used to taking care of everything related to me and my tennis that she found it harder to lead her new life. She had given up her own tennis career to support me. But as a couple, we were already drifting apart, and I felt like that was mutual. Outwardly, it looked like we were still married, travelling together while I was 'on vacation'. But the truth was, I had already moved on and started seeing other people. After tennis ended, we lived completely separate lives.

When you're a professional tennis player, it's hard to live like that. If your partner isn't with you on the road, other temptations inevitably show up, that's just how it is. Many people are drawn to tennis players for different reasons. The ones who make it work are the ones who travel together all the time.

Mariana had been a huge part of my success, part of the team. It was her, Labbe and me. Then my mum and dad behind the scenes. But I didn't let Mariana, or anyone else, have a say when it came to my decision to quit. I had been so dependent on them. My family had been my 'team'. But their only role had been to support me in my tennis and everything around it.

One grey November day in 1981 in Stockholm, I finally told my parents that I was quitting. It was incredibly hard, and I dreaded it. They already knew something was wrong, but I was certain they'd think quitting was a terrible idea. I took them out to lunch and told them the truth. Of course they thought it was awfully sad, but they also said that they understood.

Later I told Labbe. He didn't take it so well. His first reaction was to think I was joking. He was a funny guy with a special kind of humour, that was how he coped with serious things. And this was one of them.

I was selfish in quitting when I did, and that's something I can admit and regret today. Labbe knew how good I was and just wanted to help me win more titles. He was like a second father to me. But no matter how badly he wanted me to keep playing, I was the one who had to do the work. I was the one who had to step on court.

Even my sponsors were devastated. Diadora, my shoe sponsor, offered me a share of the company if I would just keep playing. Donnay and Fila were just as disappointed, everyone tried to change my mind.

Many tennis players end their careers because of injury; it allows them to cash in on insurance policies. But not me. I didn't even do that. I've never been much of a businessman. And I'd learn that the hard way soon enough. Looking back at how badly things went, how low I sank after quitting, I should have kept going a bit longer. The joy might have come back eventually. Every job has its ups and downs. But the decision was made. And nothing could change it.

In the end, I didn't betray anyone but myself. My ego is strong, and when I make up my mind, that's it. I can be stubborn to a fault. If I had just been left alone for a while, taken a longer break, who knows what might've happened?

*

After a while, Mariana moved out of the house on Long Island. She suggested we divide up the furniture, the art, and everything we'd bought over the years, but that's never been my style. I told her to take whatever she wanted. Not because we'd fought during the divorce. We were never on bad terms. I wasn't sad, she wasn't sad. We just stood there packing up the house we'd once shared. Whatever she didn't take, I left behind when we sold the place. I mostly just wanted out of New York and that whole life. What did I need that house for now? The divorce became official about a year later, but we remained friends. She kept in touch with my parents for a long time afterwards.

Mariana and I had a good time together. She's an amazing woman in many ways, deserving of all the respect in the world for putting up with that life. I don't look back on it with sadness or regret – not the marriage, the divorce, or even selling the house. I'm convinced that if I had kept playing tennis, we would still be married. My parents probably thought it was a shame we broke up, but they've always supported me no matter what. Whatever I did, they stood by it.

And just like Mariana faded out of my daily life, so did Labbe. He was still around, his fatherly presence and impact on me was still important. But when it came to this decision, I didn't let him in. He realised on his own that there was no convincing me. When it's over, it's over.

20

Life is a Party

After Mariana and I split up, I started spending more and more time in Sweden. Among other things, I spent a lot of time in Malmö, where I got the chance to train with Malmö IF, the ice hockey team that played in Sweden's top league at the time. Training was still important to me, now as a counterbalance to all the partying. Playing hockey felt familiar. It had been one of my favourite sports for as long as I could remember, and it was far enough removed from tennis that it didn't feel like work. I got to be out training on the ice with the team, which was the most fun part, after all, I'd done plenty of dry-land workouts in my career. I'm still grateful that they let me join them.

I hadn't picked up a tennis racket since early in 1982, but I did send a telegram to Mats Wilander congratulating him on his sensational win at the French Open on 6 June. At the same time, I couldn't help thinking I would've had a good chance of winning if I'd played the tournament. Otherwise, I tried not to think about tennis at all.

When I came to Stockholm, I often stayed with Labbe and his wonderful family in Saltsjö-Boo, just outside the city. My decision to quit tennis hadn't affected our relationship much, and I was still welcome in their home, almost like one of the family. But I had a restlessness in my body and wanted to be out. The nightclub Alexandra's became one of my favourite hangouts. Alexandra Charles was Sweden's queen of night-life, the Swedish equivalent of Régine in Paris. It was easy to just swing by, and you always ran into someone you knew. Alexandra ran a tight ship, and her place was one that could be counted on.

In the summer, I spent a lot of time in the US, and that's when my drug use really took off. I know it started at Studio 54, a place overflowing with white powder and everything else. The first time I tried cocaine, I got the same kind of rush I used to get from tennis. The feeling itself was new, and it made me feel incredibly energised. I was hooked immediately. The high I'd once got from tennis was gone, and now I'd found something else. I didn't realise then just how dangerous it was. With the benefit of age and hindsight, I know now how destructive it is. I was lucky I didn't go under.

So many different things were happening all the time, and one time I was lured back to Flushing Meadows for an inter-view. I was walking around alone on the grounds, waiting for the journalist to arrive. Then I saw the scoreboard; it still hadn't been reset. The numbers from my loss to John that September were still up. No one had bothered to take them down. Just seeing those numbers again gave me a wave of anxiety.

That summer, I was also invited to appear on several major

American talk shows. Everyone wanted to know what I was doing during my break from tennis, and most of all, why I wasn't playing. On 23 July 1982, I appeared on *The Tonight Show* with Johnny Carson, the biggest talk show of its time. Aside from hosting his popular show, Johnny was a huge tennis fan and had seen me win all five of my Wimbledon titles from the stands. I'd often spotted him at the US Open, too. During the interview, Johnny asked me in detail why I wasn't playing that year. I told him it was because of the tour rules, that I would've had to qualify to play the big tournaments. At the time, it was unheard of for a player to make a comeback after a break of five or six months.

It had all started a few years earlier in Boca Raton, Florida. We, the top five players in the world, had met up to push for changes to the calendar. There were far too many tournaments, and the schedule was way too intense. Back then, there was no players' union like there is now, so it was hard to get your voice heard. But together, we hoped we could apply pressure and make a difference. After hours of talks, we walked away feeling pretty satisfied. The problem was that, as the year went on, I was the only one who actually stuck to our agreement. The others kept playing as usual, and eventually I had to start qualifying for tournaments because I hadn't played enough. It was rare. I became the first player to win Monte Carlo, for example, after having to qualify just to get in.

Everyone except me probably assumed I'd be back playing Grand Slam tournaments soon. That's what I told Johnny Carson, too. To everyone who asked, I kept up the façade. I said I just needed a break, to live a little, have fun. That I'd done nothing but play tennis for so many years and just needed to rest. On the show, I said I would start playing again in September that year. I said how excited I was for next year's Wimbledon, and how maybe I'd finally win the US Open. I talked about having many more years of tennis ahead of me.

Of course, none of that was true. It wasn't just Johnny Carson's show, it was my show, too.

That summer, my dad was turning fifty, and I remember thinking he seemed so old. I flew home to Sweden and met up with a few friends of the family in the Gärdet neighbourhood in Stockholm. From there, we took a helicopter to Kättilö to celebrate his big day. That's how I lived now, a fast-paced life full of parties and nightlife around the world, even as I spent more time in Sweden.

I had no schedule. I could do whatever I wanted. I often thought to myself, 'God, this is great, I don't have to get up and train.' I wasn't living some luxurious life, even if I'd made a lot of money and even if it might've seemed like it since I was flying a helicopter from Stockholm to Kättilö. But actually, it was fairly common. There was frequent chopper traffic to and from Gärdet.

In all of 1982, I played only one real tournament, the Monte Carlo Open in April. I reached the quarter-finals before losing to Yannick Noah. I only played there out of a sense of gratitude to the club. They had always supported me, and I wanted to return the favour. I also played a few final exhibition matches and got well paid. There was still a huge demand to see me play, especially in the US. The world still hadn't had enough of me.

In January 1983, I officially announced that I was retiring from competitive tennis. The news was broadcast around the world after I told reporters at an exhibition match in South-east Asia. Rumours had been swirling for some time, and I just wanted to get it over with. By then, I had started training again, but the motivation still wasn't there.

The final official tournament I would play was again the Monte Carlo Open in April. Now that everyone knew I was retiring, the world press showed up in force. I was twenty-six years old, and this would be my last tournament. I lost to the soon twenty-year-old Henri Leconte, who would go on to become one of the stars of the new tennis generation. As I walked off the centre court, I didn't feel much of anything. It had been a good match, it went to a tiebreak in the third set. I was ready to go.

In 1983 and 1984, I agreed to play two more tournaments, one in Monte Carlo, one in Stuttgart. I was talked into playing in Stuttgart because I had won there in 1981, and they offered me two Mercedes-Benzes if I would just show up. Labbe had his eye on a new car, so I promised him one if he came along. We went, I lost in the first round, but we got the cars. And again I lost to Henri Leconte.

The rest of the time, I was completely free and thinking about what to do next. One of the many odd requests I got was to serve as a judge at a beauty pageant, Miss Hawaiian Tropic, which took place on an early summer evening in 1984 at one of Stockholm's trendy venues. One of the contestants was Jannike Björling. After the competition, we sat together at dinner and started talking. Jannike was young and still lived with her sister, but things between us got serious quickly. I thought she was refreshing, a new presence in my life, unconnected to my old tennis world.

At the time, I wasn't yet formally divorced from Mariana, so of course there was some drama when photos of Jannike and me were published around the world. Mariana wasn't thrilled to see pictures of us in the press before our divorce was finalised, and I'm sure she felt some bitterness towards me. But we both knew the relationship was over. 'When it's over, it's over,' I told myself, as I always did. That pattern has repeated itself throughout my whole life: moving on to a new love very quickly, often before the previous relationship has fully concluded. I've always needed to have someone by my side.

Jannike and I started spending more and more time together as a couple. We headed out to the Stockholm archipelago for midsummer and enjoyed the Swedish summer on a rented boat with some friends. That summer, we also stayed at the house on Long Island, and later we took a trip to Hawaii. We had to take advantage of the freedom while we had it, before anything tied us down.

I was now spending even more of my time in Sweden, and with that came other changes. In the mid-1980s, I was appointed as a tourism ambassador for Sweden. Politics had always interested me, even if I never aligned with any particular party. I've always believed in voting, it's a civic duty. So the ambassador role felt both honourable and exciting. There was a campaign called 'Discover Sweden', and the newspapers had fun trying to get me to pinpoint cities, lakes and landmarks on a map. I always declined, I thought it was a bit silly. They were clearly trying to trip me up once it became public that I'd been appointed ambassador. But my real job was to promote Sweden abroad, and in a way, I'd always done that.

In 1987, the Swedish government invited me to accompany Prime Minister Ingvar Carlsson on his official visit to the United States and the White House to meet President Ronald Reagan. It was such an eye-opening trip, to see first-hand the enormous work our politicians do. We arrived at the White House with a large entourage for a reception and dinner with invited guests, many of them Swedish-Americans. Ronald Reagan loved tennis and had always followed my career. Wilhelm Wachtmeister, Sweden's legendary ambassador to the US at the time, was involved in tennis at the Royal Tennis Club in Stockholm, and we had built a good connection through that. Later, when George H. W. Bush became President and visited Stockholm, we played tennis together, at the Royal Tennis Club, of course. We met several more times after that and even played tennis on the court at the White House. He was incredibly into the sport and once came to watch an exhibition match between me and John McEnroe in the US. I happened to win that match, and afterwards John was annoyed. He said, 'How can you beat me in front of my president?'

Back in Stockholm, I bought an apartment on Vegagatan near Odenplan where Jannike and I lived before buying a house in Vikingshill, out in the suburb of Nacka where the city met the archipelago. Eventually, we also sold the house on Long Island. I just didn't see the point of keeping it any more. My parents bought a place on the island of Värmdö in the Stockholm archipelago called Alstaholm, a manor-style villa from the turn of the century. They were constantly travelling between Sweden, Monte Carlo and Cap Ferrat.

Around that time, we also decided to let go of Kättilö. It had become too complicated to get to, and on top of that, we'd had a break-in where the thieves made off with many of my trophies and other valuables. Kättilö was remote, which had its pros and cons. Clearly, someone knew exactly where it was and when no one would be there. The thieves had free rein. The Gemini in me, who always felt at home both everywhere and nowhere, suddenly felt rootless again. My beloved getaway was now just a memory.

21

My Son and I

Jannike got pregnant, and in September 1985, my first child, Robin, was born. I couldn't have been prouder. I was, of course, thrilled when she told me she was expecting, even though we hadn't really talked seriously about having children. My feelings were entirely positive. The day Robin was born is one of the proudest moments of my life. How can you feel such boundless love for another human being? A new chapter in my life had begun: He was completely innocent and his life rested entirely in my hands.

Still, it didn't take long before Jannike and I ran into serious problems, and she went to the media accusing me of having ruined her. I still hope she regrets doing that. It was a turbulent time. We fought about everything, but the worst were the custody battles over Robin. He really got caught in the middle.

The biggest failure of my life is how absent I was during Robin's childhood. My life was pure chaos, and I couldn't always be there for him. In recent years, I've tried to make up for some of what was lost, but it's hard to undo the past. All I can say is that I wish it had been different. I'm just grateful he came through it all okay and has built a good life for himself. For me, he was the one truly good thing that came out of the 1980s.

During Robin's early years, my parents took on a huge role. They became like his second set of parents. My dad used to say he had two sons, me and Robin. That's how it felt for my parents, and probably for Robin too. They gave him the stability and sense of safety he needed growing up.

I constantly felt under attack from all directions, and I have to thank my mental strength for getting me through it. Anyone else might have considered ending it all. That's how bad it was. The media were the worst. They were always on the hunt for dirt, desperate to make headlines. I felt like they were out to destroy me. I know the tabloids thrived off me during those years, and sure, I gave them material, but the paparazzi hounded me endlessly. Thankfully it's not like that any more. Now it only happens if I'm seen with other celebrities, like when I meet up with Boris Becker. That's when they show up.

I really relate to Boris. He's made a lot of bad decisions and business deals too. But he's genuinely a good guy and a true friend. We're alike in many ways, he's also way too trusting. The problem is, if you try to go into business without the right people around you, it can go really badly. I'm so thankful that our friendship has lasted through all the chaos. I love our long conversations, just sitting and talking about everything we've been through. Boris is one of the few people I can do that with. There aren't many who can truly understand what we've experienced.

Boris calls us BB1 and BB2. I'm BB1, of course. Sometimes he'll text me: 'Hello BB1, how are you?' And even if it's been a long time since we've seen each other, when we do, we pick up right where we left off.

In 1986, I celebrated my thirtieth birthday with my parents at Alstaholm on the island of Ingerö. Around then, things in my life really began to spiral. That was also the year the custody battle over Robin began. Jannike and I both wanted full custody. Initially, I thought shared custody was best, that Robin should spend equal time with both parents. I still believe that's important for any child. But once the media smears started, we both went all in, and it got ugly, especially for Robin.

There were so many articles and interviews that never got published because someone managed to stop them in time. I was easy prey for the press, and they seemed to love writing bad things about me. It really affected me then, and still does now, more than I let on. Just like on the tennis court, I kept a poker face. Showing emotion could be a weakness the opponent would exploit.

Jannike and I fought for years. Sometimes we got along, and those were good times for Robin, just how I wanted it to be. I try to believe I did the best I could. Robin has grown into a wise man, and he understands now that I was in a difficult place. During those chaotic years, Vitas was the only person from the tennis world I stayed in touch with. No one else called or reached out, and I didn't either. I had shut myself off from it all. The phone was silent. Maybe they assumed I was fine because I didn't show otherwise. I never reached out either. They had their structured lives, a life I secretly missed. They would never have fitted into my world of parties and wild nights around the globe.

Vitas was still my best – and by then, only – friend from my tennis years. He loved coming to Stockholm. Here, he could relax and wasn't constantly recognised. We trained together at SALK Hall in Bromma, and when Jannike and I lived in Vikingshill, he stayed with us. Since he wasn't as famous in Sweden, he could go out unnoticed and party freely. He said he came to recharge, but it usually turned into partying. He was always laughing and made friends easily, even some Swedish ones, during his many visits. He knew my parents well and got along great with Robin. Since he never had children of his own, he really enjoyed being around us.

One time the three of us went to Disney World in Orlando. Robin and I flew to Florida, where Vitas was staying, and we checked into a hotel right on the park grounds and stayed for several days. We rode every ride and did everything you do with a three-year-old. Vitas loved it. Robin did too, though I think he mostly wanted to have me to himself, not share me with 'Uncle Vitas'.

A special thing Robin and I did just before the Orlando trip was go to the Tennis Hall of Fame in Newport, Rhode Island. I'd been feeling pressure to go for years since I had been inducted, which is a huge honour. It's customary to attend and give a speech, but I'd been putting it off. I never liked being the centre of attention. It wasn't the speech itself, it was the idea of being publicly celebrated like that.

Eventually, I had to do it. It's the highest honour a tennis player can receive, and it felt wrong not to go. My sixty-four career singles titles on the ATP tour still hold up pretty well today.

Robin and I flew to New York and drove to Newport. He was only three and didn't understand why we were there. But he stood with me on the court during the award ceremony when I received the glass plaque. I gave a very short thank-you speech, shorter than what's typical, but everyone was just happy I had come. The whole world was happy, and that made me happy.

Maybe it was something I needed to do for myself. I was proud of my career and wanted to show that to Robin, even if he was too young to grasp it. He always enjoyed being around the tennis world, and when he got older, he trained as often as he could in Stockholm.

I've always tried to do my best for him. When it was time for school, it felt natural that he start at Carlsson primary school in Östermalm, Stockholm. He liked it and got a good education, even though it's a demanding school. He mostly lived at Alstaholm with my parents when I wasn't around, but also with Jannike in the city. It was probably an unusual upbringing, even if many kids grow up with divorced parents.

When possible, Robin came with me to senior tournaments. He was really into tennis and played well himself, but of course he was under enormous pressure, more than Leo is now, since my career was still fresh in everyone's minds and the press was still watching everything around me.

Robin won a number of tournaments in Sweden and was among the best. His serve is killer and his forehand often carried him to victory. When he later joined me on the senior tour, he spent a lot of time with Mansour Bahrami's son, Sam. They were the same age and both played tennis. Sometimes they went to tennis camps together, like Tim Wilkison's in North Carolina.

We also spent time with Labbe, who had started working for a German company that sold travel packages to places where he held tennis clinics. These were tennis holidays where enthusiasts could improve their game. The week ended with some friendly matches. I joined in and played with the guests as much as I could, and Robin came along to train. Those weeks were great – tennis, good food and real family time. I wanted Robin to try other sports too, and we often went skiing in the mountains. But tennis won out, even for him. As he got older, he would often help warm up players on the senior tour.

Robin has always preferred smaller, quieter places. He never really felt at home in Stockholm, so he chose to attend a tennis high school in Vetlanda in the province of Småland, south-west of Stockholm. That's where he found his place, and also where he met his future wife, Sofie, though they didn't get together until a few years later.

Robin and I played each other in an exhibition match in 2004, right there in Vetlanda, with the whole family present to watch. It was a fun, close match, followed by a lovely evening and dinner. Robin won the match, and earned everyone's respect, especially since he had helped organise the whole event. Maybe that laid the groundwork for his future career, which now includes a few different roles, but primarily he works as a hockey agent. For a while, he managed the Swedish branches of Head and Diadora. He's a real entrepreneur. But above all, he's a devoted husband to Sofie and a loving father to two amazing girls, my granddaughters Céline and Allie. I'm so happy and proud that, despite all the difficult circumstances of his childhood, he found his way in life.

22

My Businesses

I had shown the world that I could play tennis and had made quite a bit of money. Not even close to what players earn today, but still a good amount for that time.

Most of what I earned over the years came from sponsorship deals, maybe even the majority. I was, and still am, good at negotiating payment for my tennis and contracts. But when it came to business in general, I was never a natural businessman. I often ended up doing the wrong thing. I have friends who are great at business, driven, almost cold in their approach. I think you have to be that way. I, on the other hand, mix in too much emotion, and I don't take business seriously enough. That mix just isn't profitable.

I like haggling because it reminds me of sport, giving your best against an opponent. But then I often end up paying more anyway, because I feel like I've already 'won'. And I've always been overly generous with tips, almost foolishly so. I've always felt like I owed everyone something. That because I made so much in my career, I had to pay it back somehow.

Honestly, I don't care much about money. I didn't have any growing up, and when I did, I never really got involved in it. I was just focused on tennis. And in many ways, I'm still that same simple guy. When people tell me I can afford a luxurious life, I just want to stay home, eat good home-cooked food, watch TV and exercise. If there's one thing I've learned, it's that I function best when life is in balance.

Finding that balance, and a new role in life, isn't easy after a life in elite sport. It's something I share with a lot of other former athletes. What do you do when your career ends? How do you stay in touch with those you once travelled and played with, those who know what that life was like?

Everyone wanted to become a businessman after their playing days. But not everyone had a talent for it. For me, it started as something to fill the void. Then it moved fast, I was pretty much thrown into the business world. I was looking for a new life, and there were plenty of people eager to pitch ideas to me and get me to invest. When I see a photo of myself from that time, in a suit with a briefcase in hand, I don't even understand why I did it, because it really wasn't me. Sure, I've had fancy homes, fast cars and loud boats, but I've always preferred peace and quiet at home. For me there's nothing more boring than shopping for things, especially clothes. I usually wear sportswear from Fila. And since no other logos are allowed to show, I just stick to Fila. Otherwise, I go for plain, neutral brands, and I'll wear the same clothes year after year. I've never been the kind of person who wants to show off, I'd rather disappear into the crowd.

My boat, *Dunderburken*, was definitely a flashy indulgence I treated myself to. Boats aren't great investments, but I had a couple built and enjoyed them immensely. *Dunderburken* was built in Valdemarsvik and made a hell of a racket, it was loud and fast, and sailors hated it when we zoomed past.

Back then, I spent time with King Carl XVI Gustaf and the prominent Swedish businessman Aje Philipson, who both shared my passion for boats and didn't mind the noise. Queen Silvia, on the other hand, thought the boat was unbearably loud. One time, Aje and the king came to my family home at Alstaholm, and my mum had to make lunch for us. She's not easily impressed, but I think she got a bit nervous when she saw the king sitting at her table.

There was a private powerboat race once, where a few of us were supposed to go from the Sandhamn of my childhood summers to the Almagrundet lighthouse which stood alone 35 kilometres away in the middle of the Baltic and back again. We were doing nearly 70 knots, and just as we were rounding the lighthouse, a gust of wind lifted the boat straight up. For a few terrifying seconds, we didn't know if we'd flip forwards or backwards.

Luckily, it landed the right way. But I was scared out of my mind and took the boat at snail's pace all the way home. It could've ended very badly.

My life as a businessman really began while I was still an active tennis player. I got a lot of offers to lend my name to different brands. I agreed to some of them, but I drew the line when it came to tobacco, alcohol and gambling. I didn't want to promote those things.

After I retired, I'd already started my own company, though I wasn't sure what to do with it. But the business proposals kept coming. I met all kinds of people pitching ideas. Two of them were Lars Skarke and Egon Håkanson, who ran a company called Project House. They specialised in sponsorship, and I soon tied all my business dealings to them. I saw an opportunity to live off my name and the goodwill I'd built from my tennis career. Lots of companies wanted to create clothes and perfumes with my name on them, but we chose to partner with the family-run company Romella. With Jack Rothschild leading the way, Romella became the agent for fragrances and cosmetics under the Björn Borg name. They were based in Stockholm and got the rights to sell the products worldwide. French designer Pierre Dinand was brought in to create a stylish look, and the result was the first truly serious products under my name. I felt proud when I saw those elegant perfume bottles. I wanted more.

So Lars Skarke and I launched a new company together, mostly with borrowed money. The idea was that my name would generate big profits. We also agreed on a stock options deal involving my old company. Skarke became my closest business partner, and around 1984, Björn Gullström joined us. He'd been my financial advisor for years, and I trusted him completely. I'd met him through financier Marcus Wallenberg, and he even helped advise my parents. We were close, and my whole family saw him as a friend. On Gullström's advice, I signed a power of attorney that gave Skarke the authority to run the business without needing my approval for every little decision. It felt like a relief. I wasn't interested in all the details, and I was still young.

But if there's one thing I wish I could undo, it's that. Signing over that power and giving Skarke so much influence over my affairs. I was too naïve. It might seem like I didn't care about the business, but that's not true. I was more involved than one would've thought, I just didn't know what I was doing.

At first, things with Skarke felt fine. I was travelling a lot, and business decisions often had to be made quickly. When we did meet, we had fun together. I've got good memories from that time, like when we played ball hockey with a group of friends. Another time, we took a luxury ski trip to St Moritz. We stayed in a five-star hotel with incredible views, enjoyed great skiing, delicious food, and partied in the evenings. Robin came along – he was little then – and we stayed together in one of the fancy rooms. That was usually the case when he travelled with me: we shared a room, and I never brought anyone else to take care of him.

After a few days of skiing and partying, I'd had enough and wanted to leave. I had to think of Robin. Skarke and the others wanted to stay, which wasn't surprising since they weren't paying for anything themselves.

The hotel staff helped me quickly book a helicopter to Nice, where my parents were. I shouldn't have done that, since the journey over the Alps was terrifying. The winds picked up violently, and the helicopter was tossed around like a feather amongst the steep mountains. I was sure we were going to crash. I don't think I've ever been so scared in my entire life. Thankfully, Robin was too young to understand what was happening. I'll never forget the relief I felt when I saw the Mediterranean and realised the worst was over. We had made it. My parents were waiting at the airport in Nice. It felt so good to leave Robin in their loving care.

Over time, Skarke took on more and more control of my business. IMG, who had been my most important advisors since 1974, were still in the background, but since I wasn't playing much any more, we didn't work together so closely.

I kept believing the business would do well, even thrive, and I wasn't the only one who bought into everything Skarke said and did. In some ways, he was good for business, at least in the short term. He had a talent for persuasion and could easily get people on board. There was always a need for more and more money to make the big expansion dreams come true. The idea was to launch a full clothing line: jackets, coats, shirts, sweaters, trousers. We hired staff, opened a flashy office on Nybrogatan in Stockholm, and planned for years while the money kept pouring out of the company. It was money I'd earned from tennis and all the sponsorships and PR events I'd done.

We brought in Swedish designer Rohdi Heintz as the head of design. He was incredibly talented, and people still talk about the collections he created for the Björn Borg brand. Soon we started testing the underwear market, and it went better than expected. We launched new products, including women's underwear and swimwear. Everything looked promising. Customers and the fashion industry loved our stuff. It was trendy, and everyone wanted it.

The problem, and it was a big one, was that nothing behind the scenes worked as it should. None of us had real experience running a clothing company at that scale. We ran into logistical problems everywhere and couldn't meet the huge demand. No matter how much we sold, clothes or underwear, the company kept bleeding money and we had to keep pouring more in. I honestly don't remember all the business deals and partnerships clearly, it was all happening so fast. Sometimes it was a dinner meeting, other times a connection led to another contact. Sure, we were living large at the time, but I felt like I deserved it after all those hard years on the tennis court. I wanted to make up for lost time. The only problem was that none of the other people involved had ever been world number one in tennis.

Out of all these ventures came the creation of the Björn Borg Design Group. That's where the money from my PR work was funnelled. The goal was to take control of the brand and continue expanding globally. In 1988, we officially launched the company in Monte Carlo with a big event at the Monte

Carlo Tennis Club. It was a huge moment for me, I'd spent so much time at that club since 1972. I thought my business career was really about to take off. And in some ways, it did. New offices opened around the world. The underwear line was so hot that high-end department stores created special Björn Borg sections.

But it still wasn't working out. We couldn't get a handle on our cash flow, and the company kept bleeding money. It felt like a downward spiral, like being caught in a wave that keeps pulling you under. I'd already invested so much of my own money that I felt I had to keep going just to get something back.

One of my strongest memories from that time is the fax machine at the house in Vikingshill. It never stopped churning out pages of business updates, day and night. It had its own room with the door closed because of the noise. When it was time to change the paper roll, it was almost impossible to open the door, it was so stuffed with pages. But I kept changing the roll anyway, just so more faxes could come through. I don't even know why I bothered. Maybe I just needed to feel like I had some kind of control while everything else was falling apart. One thing's for sure: I wasn't thinking clearly, and I didn't have time to read every message.

No profit was being generated, and things looked worse by the day. A divide started forming in the company. The one group I could always count on was IMG. They'd been warning me for a while and wanted me to stop. But I hadn't listened. My internal warning bells never went off, and I just kept going. Now they strongly advised me against putting in more funds.

By February 1989, I realised my friend Gullström had switched, as tensions inside the company turned into an open conflict. Gullström and I had always worked well together, so his betrayal hit me hard. He acted as if he'd been brainwashed, he didn't seem to care that I was left all alone, stuck paying out of my own pocket.

When Gullström abandoned me, I knew deep down that it was over. The house of cards collapsed, and I was left alone.

On 27 July 1989, the company went bankrupt. It left me with massive personal debts, and the house in Vikingshill had to be sold at a foreclosure auction. In the end, I had to cover a huge part of the losses myself, bank loans and debts the company had racked up over the years.

Losing the house wasn't even the worst of it. In some ways, it was a relief. It had started to feel haunted, like it had some dark energy. The apartment on Vegagatan and my boat, *Dunderburken*, were also lost in the bankruptcy. I had no choice but to accept it. I'd always wanted to do right by people, but now I felt completely inadequate, like no one had my back. Everyone was after me: debt collectors, journalists, and everyone else involved like lawyers and former employees.

At the same time the business was collapsing, I was on the verge of making my next huge mistake, marrying my new love, the Italian singer Loredana Bertè. My drug problems also worsened during this period. I'm not blaming anyone, but I needed an escape. I figured, 'why not go inwards?' At least that way I wouldn't hurt anyone else. But that was the wrong path, completely selfish. Because that kind of escape does hurt others, and badly. The ones who suffered most were the people closest to me, my son Robin and my parents.

23

My Demons Make
an Appearance

The first time I tried drugs was in the summer of 1982, during that so-called break from tennis when I was killing time in New York. At first, it was just about having fun, letting loose. I didn't know any better, and a lot of people around me were doing it. Eventually, it became more of a habit, a way to deal with the dark thoughts that had started creeping in. It was simply an escape, a way to step into a lighter, more carefree bubble. And of course, I got stuck in it.

I've always believed in astrology, and Gemini is supposed to be one of the most complicated signs. Sometimes it feels like I'm made up of two different people, one good and one bad. Just as easily as I can feel full of life, I can also be impulsive and behave almost self-destructively. I've never been comfortable being alone with my own thoughts, it's like they come rushing at me. That's when the demons catch up, and that's when the self-medicating starts. But that's obviously not the right way to deal with it, because once you've tamed one addiction, another one just takes its place.

People have always said I didn't show much emotion, but inside it was a rollercoaster. I never talked about how I was really doing, not with friends, not with other tennis players. They never said how they were doing, and neither did I.

There just wasn't the same openness back then about these kinds of issues. I didn't have mental coaches or psychologists working with me. Things are probably better now, but when I recently watched the documentary about Mardy Fish, the American tennis player who had to stop playing because of severe anxiety, it all came flooding back.

The documentary tells the story of his battle with mental health and how his friend Andy Roddick tried to help him. Fish and Roddick carried the weight of being the great hope of American tennis in the early 2000s, but Fish's anxiety became so overwhelming that his body just shut down. He had to walk away from tennis when he couldn't even step onto the court to face Roger Federer at the US Open.

Tennis is a lonely sport, and it takes its toll, but for me, it was never on the court that I felt bad. It was everything around it. Even today, I can feel completely drained just from signing autographs or dealing with people who want something from me. It's made me hide away indoors for long stretches at a time.

My relationships haven't just followed one another, they've also overlapped. If I didn't have someone, I made sure I found someone. I just couldn't handle being alone, not even for a second, and I'll admit that. I never really ended one relationship properly before another one began, or more accurately, I never dared end one unless someone new was already lined up. As soon as a relationship started falling apart, I was already looking for the next one. Most of the time, I looked for love within my own circle, like with Mariana from the tennis world, or at parties with friends. It was harder to meet someone out at a bar or club, because everyone knew who I was. So sometimes it just came down to chance, who I happened to meet, who became my new sense of security. Looking back, it almost feels random who I ended up with, whoever happened to be closest. A few times I even got back in touch with old girlfriends, just so I wouldn't be alone. It was easier with someone familiar, someone within reach. The most important thing was that it was easy.

I had met Loredana Bertè back in the '70s in New York, when she was dating the Italian tennis player Adriano Panatta. Much later, when things got really bad at home in Sweden with Jannike, I escaped to Italy to visit friends. I just wanted peace and quiet, but as usual, I quickly felt lonely and reached out to Loredana. She had always kind of been in the periphery of my social circle.

And then it happened again, the same pattern. I got involved with Loredana before things were officially over with Jannike, just like I'd met Jannike before my divorce from Mariana was finalised. If I'd known then what was coming, I would have done things completely differently. But once again, my impulsiveness and fear of being alone led me down the wrong path. For someone like me, already struggling with drugs and pills, the scene in Milan turned out to be completely destructive. That was the beginning of a truly dark chapter in my life.

24

The Dark Years in Milan

I love Italy. I love the people, the country, the culture and the food, but my 'escape' there was mostly a way to get away from everything that was going on back home. And as usual, I thought meeting someone new would solve things. That it would somehow change everything.

When Loredana and I met in Milan, things went so well between us that I extended my stay. We got an invitation to go to Ibiza, and we went. On the island, we stayed in a private villa, swimming, sunbathing and eating out all the time. Everything felt amazing, and we were in that early honeymoon phase.

Loredana and I kept prolonging our trip and ended up staying quite a while. She was at the peak of her career, and everyone knew who she was, a talented Italian singer who wasn't afraid of anything. She dressed however she wanted and said whatever she felt like saying – she was wonderfully outspoken.

The funny thing is, a lot of the people we met back then are still in Ibiza. Every now and then, I'll bump into old acquaintances. When Patricia and I went back to Ibiza years later, someone recommended this Italian restaurant up in the mountains. We went, and when the owner saw me, he actually started crying. 'I knew you'd come back!' he said. Apparently, he remembered me better than I remembered most of that trip.

When the vacation ended, we returned to Milan and I moved into Loredana's apartment. Not long after, we got engaged.

I was never officially registered in Milan, even though I mostly lived there. There was probably something subconscious holding me back from making a permanent move. I missed my parents sometimes, but it only took about three hours to drive to Monte Carlo or Cap Ferrat. I could leave in the morning, have lunch with them, and head back afterward. Sometimes I stayed a few nights to get a bit of peace and quiet away from all the chaos in Milan.

I spent a lot of time trying to convince Loredana to move with me to Monte Carlo, where I still had an apartment. But she flat-out refused. She was on her home turf in Milan. In Monte Carlo, there was a network around me that surely would have noticed and stepped in once they realised how badly I was doing.

We got married in 1989 in Italy. The wedding was small, and we had both a civil and a church ceremony. It was held in a Protestant church in Milan, followed by dinner at a restaurant. Nothing like my previous wedding. There was no bachelor party – I didn't have any friends left, either from my tennis days or from the business world. I'd burned all those bridges. On my side, it was just my mum, dad, grandma Greta, grandpa Martin, and of course, Robin. He was four years old and probably didn't understand much of what was going on, he just ran around playing among the adult guests.

I think my parents saw early on that this was a disaster

waiting to happen, that I was heading down the wrong path. But they were overwhelmed dealing with the mess from my failing businesses and the bankruptcy. They couldn't do much more.

The marriage was more of a concession on my part, and deep down, I hoped it might work out. My life had got so tangled: business problems, custody issues with Robin, everything. Loredana also wanted to have children with me, which I can understand – she was six years older than I was. It even went as far as me going to a clinic to leave a sperm sample for insemination. I just went along with it.

During those years in Milan, life turned into a chaotic mess. There were moments of light and deep darkness, but always turmoil. I never knew what mood Loredana would be in when I woke up, whether it would be a good day or a bad one. Meanwhile, the arguments with Jannike continued, so I came up with the not-so-brilliant idea that Robin should come live with me and Loredana. That's what we did, and I enrolled him in an international preschool in Milan, surrounded by unfamiliar kids speaking strange languages.

It didn't take long to realise it wasn't working. Robin was clearly sad and confused, and I was filled with anxiety every morning when I put him on the school bus. We stuck it out for a while, but eventually it became unsustainable, and he moved back to Sweden, where Jannike and my parents took care of him. I still carry a lot of shame for putting Robin through that, especially from when I was bringing him to Milan. When we talk about it now, Robin says he's moved on and doesn't like looking back.

When things fall apart, it's never just one person's fault. I obviously played my part in how everything turned out. I surrounded myself with the wrong people, and drugs and pills were always within reach. This is where I hit absolute rock bottom, and I didn't want to be there any more. I felt worse and worse. It became a vicious cycle of exhaustion and anxiety. I just thought: I can't take this any more. I'm done.

One early morning in February 1989, Loredana couldn't wake me up, and she called an ambulance. The fact that I'm still alive is thanks to her, for calling for help and getting me to the hospital, where they pumped my stomach. That turned into global headlines as a suicide attempt. But it wasn't that. I never intended to end my life. Even though I didn't want to live like that any more, I never made a conscious decision to end everything.

What happened was that I had a dangerous mix of drugs, pills and alcohol in my system, and it knocked me out. In a way, maybe it was a cry for help. I survived, and I was deeply grateful for that. When I came home from the hospital, I realised my life had spun completely out of control, and for a while, I actually took it a bit easier on the drugs. But then the weeks went by. The demons returned. New things happened, and soon I was back where I started. I hated it. I was completely drained, I knew I couldn't keep living like this for ever. So while the overdose wasn't some sudden turning point, a desire for change did start to grow inside me. I realised I had to get out of the marriage if I wanted to survive.

Once again, I felt the need to escape from everything, to leave both Milan and Loredana. The only way out that I could think of, the only thing I knew, was to start playing tennis again. Sure, that came with its own anxiety, but it was my last lifeline.

Loredana is also an entire chapter in my life, but it's one that's hard to talk about because I have so many bad memories from my time in Milan. Our divorce wasn't finalised until 1993, and by then, we hadn't had any contact in a long time. But even to this day, she has caused me problems.

25

The Comeback

Early in 1990, maybe even as a kind of New Year's resolution, I started thinking about introducing some structure into my life in Milan. I realised it was the only way I was going to survive. The drugs had taken over, and I had to pull the emergency brake. Sure, I'd been continuing to stay in shape by running and using my exercise bike, but that training wasn't enough. The most natural thing was to return to what I'd always done: play tennis.

I knew that a talented Swedish tennis player, Jonas Svensson, was living in Milan and I reached out to him and asked if he'd be willing to train with me. Fortunately, he agreed, and we began playing a few times a week. At the start I was completely worn down, both physically and mentally. My tennis wasn't exactly pretty, but I kept at it. Slowly but surely, a spark was reignited, a flicker of life after a long time in the dark.

I also felt a strong need to get away from the people around me. Some of them clearly didn't have my best interests at heart.

I started thinking about trying to get to London. I still had good contacts there from the past, and I figured I could probably feel somewhat at home. Loredana wasn't surprised by my plan, and we agreed that I should go.

I left, packing only what I really needed: rackets, shoes and clothes. I checked into one of the most luxurious hotels in the city, a place I'd stayed many times before. That became my personal rehab centre and my base for the foreseeable future. I was determined to return to some kind of routine, so I contacted the Queen's Club in London. They were incredibly supportive and put together a tennis programme for me so I could train every day with the best players in the UK.

Once there, the hard work of rebuilding myself began. I didn't let anyone from my old life get close to me. And there were plenty of them, not just in Italy, but all over the world. People who wanted to party, jump aboard the wild ride, or score free drugs. It was like an invisible network – wherever I went, they could find me and make sure the drugs were there. So-called friends who didn't care about me at all. I had money, didn't care much about it, and always ended up footing the bill. The money slipped through my fingers like water.

Loredana actually visited me a few times during that period. She'd stay a couple of days and then head back to Milan. She didn't interfere with my set-up, I was totally focused on my recovery, but I think she got bored, and eventually the visits stopped altogether. I didn't see Robin at all during this time, which was tough. I didn't see my parents either, because if they came to visit, there would be dinners and socialising, and that meant alcohol, and from there it was a short slide back to drugs.

Word got out that I was in London, and yes, some articles were written. But no one really knew why I was there. I'd already withdrawn from public life. Every year I was invited as a guest to the major tournaments, especially Wimbledon and the French Open, but I never showed up. I was too worn out, nowhere near ready to face people or journalists, because I knew they'd have a thousand questions about what I'd been doing and where I'd been. So I stayed as isolated as possible, just the hotel and the tennis club.

Looking back, it's kind of amazing that nothing leaked about my time in rehab. I was still a prime target for the British tabloids, and the smallest thing usually became a headline. The people helping me in London were incredibly loyal, and I was given the chance I needed to recover in peace and quiet.

I stayed at the hotel for quite a while. I played some of the worst tennis of my life, but that didn't matter. I was alive and I wanted to come back. I still had a decent fitness base from Milan, and maybe that's what saved me, both there and at other points in my life. I'd pretty much always trained, even in my darkest times. I never put on weight, and for the most part I managed to stop myself before things got out of hand.

At the hotel in London, I made sure every day was exactly like the one before. Nothing could change. Everything had to follow the strict routine I had created. I'd wake up early, have breakfast in my room, then head to the tennis club for a couple of hours of training. I usually had lunch at the club with whichever player I'd trained with. We didn't talk about the match or the game, we just chatted like normal people. Sometimes I preferred to eat alone, in which case I'd quickly head back to the hotel. In the afternoon, I'd train again for a few hours, then go back, take a shower, collapse on the bed, order room service, watch some TV and fall asleep early.

Day by day, I rebuilt myself. I'd created this completely closed-off system where nothing and no one could get to me.

Labbe was no longer involved in my training, but during my time in London I started visiting a particular 'guru' more frequently. His name was Tia Honsai, he called himself a professor, and I'd met him way back in 1978 when I was playing at Wimbledon. He was sort of a healer, and to this day I'm not entirely sure what he did. He just used his hands in some sort of healing process. Our family friend Erik Steiner knew him, and one time, when I had a bit of an injury, Erik brought me to Honsai's practice in a London villa. Labbe came with me that first time in '78, and even he noticed something had changed after the session. Honsai touched me, the pain disappeared, and my energy increased dramatically. I walked out of there feeling like Superman. After that, I returned to Tia Honsai regularly whenever I was in London.

I've always been open to alternative treatments and I believe in some form of inner healing. Even if there's some placebo effect involved, I like to believe that not everything requires drastic medical solutions. The rumour eventually spread that I had met the 'guru'. I was the first among the tennis players to go, but soon others followed in my footsteps.

As summer and Wimbledon approached, I started missing my family more, my parents and Robin. I left London, not really having a fixed base, and bounced between Stockholm and Cap Ferrat, spending time with the people I cared about. Loredana was now completely out of the picture. We no longer saw each other at all.

My physical and mental strength was slowly returning, but I wasn't done. That autumn, I went back to London and resumed the same training routine. I still wanted to improve my tennis, even though I knew I wouldn't return to my peak level. I got the same room at my hotel, and they welcomed me back.

When I finally felt well enough to leave the hotel in London, I headed south and spent most of my time in Cap Ferrat. There, I had time to reflect on everything that had happened, and all that I'd forsaken. My loved ones had been hit hard by my time in Milan. Robin hadn't had a real father for a long while, he'd either been with my parents or with Jannike. My parents, who I'd always been so close to, hadn't known exactly where I was for a long time, just that I was in London, that I was safe, needed to get away from my old life and be in peace. So I had some work to do in rebuilding my life.

Thinking back on Milan filled me with anxiety. That whole period was a blur, full of both intentional and unintentional memory gaps. In Cap Ferrat, I found a bit of peace, and tennis was an important part of that balance. I trained like I had in London, and sometimes, the idea of playing in a tournament again crept in. Rumours started swirling that I was thinking of a comeback. The tennis world began reaching out, and soon I had lots of offers through my agent at IMG. At the same time, a familiar feeling returned, the desire to give something back after everything I'd received during my tennis years.

I turned down most of the tournament invitations straight away. There was still a bit of resistance in me, because I knew that the moment I said yes, there would be no turning back. But after some persuasion, I decided to play 'at home' on the clay in Monte Carlo, at the ATP tournament in April 1991. That club had always supported me, so it felt like the natural choice.

This was going to be the so-called comeback, and the news made headlines around the world. Everyone called it a comeback, but for me, it wasn't about that. I just wanted to have some fun and show that I had managed to come back to life. To me, it was a miracle that, with the help of some higher power, I'd made it out of hell. At the same time, I was curious to play a match again, to feel what the old life was like. I didn't talk about any of this publicly, and a lot of people thought I was nuts for staging a comeback at one of the biggest tournaments instead of starting at a smaller event.

In the beginning of 1991, I also got an invitation to play an exhibition tournament in Houston, Texas. It was held in River Oaks, a very exclusive area with a beautiful, historic tennis club. I decided to play there as well, ahead of the Monte Carlo comeback. The tournament always attracted the top-ranked Swedish players. I liked the idea of spending time with the other Swedes again, to feel that Swedish camaraderie I'd missed on so many occasions. That year, Mats Wilander, Mikael Pernfors and Peter Lundgren were among those playing in Houston. We had so many top players then, and lots of others were there too – we had a great time. The tournament was played outdoors on clay, which was the perfect preparation for Monte Carlo.

The centre court in Houston was packed with an enthusiastic crowd, and I was seriously nervous walking onto the court. Winning didn't matter to me, but I didn't want to embarrass myself either. The crowd didn't see how I felt about my tennis, it was all in my head. When the match started, I didn't play well, but I won my first-round match. I lost in the second round, but still, it was fun to have made it that far.

In the crowd that day was a woman named Kari Bernhardt and her entourage. That evening, I was introduced to her. It wasn't unusual; someone from the tournament would often say: 'There are a few girls who'd like to meet you later.'

Kari came back the next day too, and saw me lose. But we all went out together, and one thing led to another. I was curious, I won't deny it, a new girl, and from the US no less. Could she be something new in my life?

I stayed in Houston for a week and spent a lot of time with

Kari. Then it was time to return to Monte Carlo and get ready for the ATP tournament. Kari and I stayed in touch, and later that autumn, I saw her again in Houston. That was the start of our long, on-and-off relationship.

The buzz around Monte Carlo didn't die down, and before the tournament, the media presence was overwhelming. The draw was held at the Sporting Club in Monte Carlo, and I was escorted in with a man on either side. One was Prince Albert, the other was Alain Delon. Together, they placed the slip with my name into the draw bowl. Everyone was curious to see who would have the honour of playing me in the first round.

The player drawn ended up being Jordi Arrese from Spain, who probably didn't know whether to laugh or cry. He certainly wasn't used to this level of attention, especially not for a first-round match. He was the clear favourite to win, but I was the crowd's favourite.

In the days leading up to the match, I trained with two young superstars: Boris Becker and Goran Ivanišević. Everything felt good, the training was in my system. In fact, they had to take turns playing with me because I apparently wore them out, one after the other. Or at least that's what I was told later by their coach, Bob Brett. That said, I wasn't match-ready in the slightest – mentally preparing for a real match is something entirely different from practice.

When I walked onto the centre court to a packed stadium, I already felt like a winner. The crowd stood and applauded. Even my parents and Labbe were there. Everyone was cheering, clearly happy to see me back on the court. But they must've been wondering how I'd hold up against this new generation of players, especially someone like Jordi Arrese.

The match started, but it was over pretty quickly. I hadn't had any real expectations, and I lost fairly easily, as expected. Not even the guru Honsai, who was sitting courtside, could perform a miracle. To be honest, he slept through the entire match. Arrese was clearly the better player, and I lost in straight sets.

But I was pleased all the same. The comeback was about reclaiming my life, and I had won that match. This was my show. And for the first time in a very long time, I was happy as I climbed into the car and drove home to Cap Ferrat with my parents.

26

Guardian Angel

It's hard to explain why someone relapses. For me, it often happened because the opportunity presented itself. Drugs would suddenly be around me without me even seeking them out. It could start with a simple dinner and a couple of drinks, and then things would spiral. And once I caught wind of the drugs, that was it, I was completely fixated on it for the rest of the night. I couldn't stop myself. There was never an in-between.

A few days after the tournament in Monte Carlo, we flew to Stockholm to get away from the media frenzy.

Despite the loss in Monte Carlo, more tournaments followed. I didn't care at all about the results. For me, it was about staying focused and playing in a more professional way. That helped me stick to my routines and keep feeling grateful that I had my life back.

The only thing I really missed was companionship. During my active career, Labbe had always been by my side, so I asked my dad if he'd be willing to travel with me. He said yes. That meant the world to me, to have my closest friend with me in that wandering lifestyle. We had a great time, and he enjoyed getting away too, treating himself to the travels and the hotel room service. It was just the two of us, my mum didn't come along during that time. My dad was my rock, and deep down I think he knew I needed support, someone to watch over me. He knew about the drugs, even though we never spoke about it, and I never used around him. Not until one fateful day in the Netherlands, sometime in the mid-'90s.

As hooked as I'd been on drugs over the years, I always stayed far away from performance enhancing drugs. That was never my thing, I was strict about it. Not just because I thought it was morally wrong, but because I wanted full control over my body and my training. During my professional career, I was extremely careful about what I put into myself. No one really knew what those substances might do in the long term. So I played it safe and tried to get what I needed through a balanced diet. Others weren't as cautious, they were more naive about it, and many doped heavily.

The risk of getting caught was practically zero. Neither I nor anyone else were tested for steroids at the time. So in a way, I can understand why it was tempting for others to get a little help. It wasn't until a tournament in San Francisco in 1992 that I was tested for the first time. Honestly, it felt like a relief, that the tennis world was finally catching up and starting to enforce regular testing.

Even now, I think it's great that players are tested. There should probably be even more of it, especially in junior tennis. There's a lot of cheating at that age, both with banned substances and by falsifying players' ages in passports. The longer you can claim to be a junior, the easier it is to attract sponsorships and lucrative deals.

*

In 1993, my friend Jimmy Connors started a senior tour. At first, it only took place in the US, but eventually it expanded to other countries as well. I became part of it, and we could be on the road up to seven or eight months a year, often in three-week stretches. During those periods, we were all really disciplined. Even though my so-called comeback career hadn't been particularly successful, I had found joy in both life and tennis again. It felt right, and fun, to be part of this new adventure. It was also a good way to keep up my training and lifestyle routines, and I'd reconnected with several of my old friends, like John McEnroe.

Plus, it paid well. Senior tennis had really taken off, both in the US and globally. Everyone wanted to see the old stars play, we were the ones who had kicked off the whole tennis boom. I was one of the biggest draws, though John McEnroe was probably better at negotiating his fee than I was.

We were incredibly serious, but we also had a lot of fun. We trained, we competed, and we joked around constantly. I remember one tournament in Tokyo where I played well and made it to the singles final, where I lost to Connors. But I won the entire doubles event with Henri Leconte. We had a blast on court, and a few nights we went out. One evening we ran into a group of American girls and invited them to come and watch tennis. They showed up to the matches, and we gave them the full VIP experience, showed them around everywhere, even brought them into the locker rooms.

That made the organisation furious, especially since we were in Japan, where they're very strict about these things. In the end, part of my prize money was deducted because I hadn't behaved as I should. I accepted the fine without complaint. It was worth it.

*

Kari and I were officially in a relationship by then, though we still lived in different places and often went long stretches without seeing each other. My dad was still travelling with me on the tennis trips, but when he needed to be home, Kari would come along instead.

By 1993, Houston had basically become my new home base. I moved into Kari's apartment. Houston is a cool city, and one of my Swedish friends, Niclas Kroon, lived there too. He was another of the many talented Swedish tennis players at the time. Every morning we'd play tennis, then grab lunch together. Some days we'd head over to Dave & Buster's to bowl, shoot pool, play darts and maybe have a beer or two.

I liked the lifestyle. I had a pretty good life in Houston, even if it never felt entirely like home. Kari lived a more hectic life, while I had grown used to taking things slow. Our on-and-off set-up worked for me. When I was away on tour, I had no idea what she was up to, and the same went for her when I was home.

So it came as a shock when Kari suddenly said she wanted to move to Los Angeles to pursue a career in Hollywood. I was hesitant. I knew the city well and knew how dangerous it could be when it came to excess. Vitas and I had been there more than a few times. But I gave in, again. She wanted to live near Beverly Hills, and eventually we found a nice apartment about ten minutes from Rodeo Drive.

As time went on, especially after the move to LA, partying started to creep back into my life again, just as I had feared. I was still travelling a lot for tennis, but when I would return after a while on the tour, it was easy to lose direction. Kari had a lot of friends in the city and was always busy. I, on the other hand, ended up more and more often at the Playboy Mansion with my old friend Hugh Hefner and a rotating cast of guests. The place was full of temptations of every kind, and it was hard to say no.

I also played some senior events in Europe, now that the tour had expanded there too. Between matches, I'd usually take the opportunity to visit my parents in Sweden and spend time with Robin. He split his time between Jannike and my parents and went to school in Stockholm. We were living worlds apart, on opposite sides of the Atlantic. It's awful to think about now. But during school breaks, he sometimes came to visit me in the US.

Then, during one of the usual European tournaments, what wasn't supposed to happen happened. I completely lost control again. The usual dinners with wine triggered other habits, and in the end, it all became too much. My body just gave out.

Beep. Beep. I woke up in a hospital room, tubes attached to my body. Where was I? At first, I remembered nothing. My dad was standing next to me, just looking at me. 'How are you doing?' I remember him saying. His wide-eyed stare was both concerned and completely blank at the same time.

As I came to, the memories slowly started returning. I had collapsed on the way to a tennis match. I was supposed to play the final of an exhibition tournament in Holland. It happened on a bridge near the venue. Someone had called an ambulance, and they had taken me in. The memories sharpened bit by bit as I lay there in the hospital bed, and it was not a pleasant experience.

To this day, I'm ashamed just thinking about it. That was the worst shame of all, that my drug problem had reached such a level, with such serious consequences, and all in front of my own father. I didn't even ask the doctors or nurses how close I'd come to dying. I didn't want to know. If you've ever seen a dog look ashamed, that's how I felt, only a hundred times worse. To think that my dad had to see me like that, hooked up to tubes and surrounded by beeping machines. He must have been terrified. Mum was probably even more anxious since she was far away, but she surely knew everything. She and Dad were always talking on the phone.

As soon as I was allowed to leave the hospital, we flew home to Stockholm. It was the worst trip I've ever taken. My dad didn't speak to me. Not when I was in the hospital, when I was discharged, not at the hotel when we went back to pack, not at the airport, not once during the entire flight home. He didn't say a single word. He was probably angry, sad, disappointed, and I just wanted to escape from the whole situation.

When we got home by taxi from the airport, Mum was waiting for me. I could tell she was disappointed. She was probably also scared about what might have happened. But then, as usual, they wanted to keep it quiet, keep it within the family, and preferably not talk about it. That's how it was in our family, nothing was to be revealed, and they didn't offer to help me with any kind of treatment for the drugs. That was something I had to handle on my own.

There's a lingering sadness inside me that I couldn't talk to Dad about what happened in Holland – not then, and never afterward. We, who otherwise shared everything, didn't even know how to begin discussing it. All I know is that it was my absolute rock bottom. Later, I learned that things could've ended much worse. I was saved because kind people nearby had made sure I got help quickly. Maybe it was my guardian angel reaching out once again.

27

A Decade Lost

Looking back, the 1990s feel like one long stretch of wasted time. If only I could turn back the clock and do something meaningful with those years. Professionally, at least, one positive thing came out of that period: Jimmy Connors starting the senior tour. That allowed me to reclaim a little of my old life, or at least the best parts of it. As a bonus, I got back in touch with my old tennis buddies. That's something I'm truly happy about.

Still, I tended to make the same mistakes over and over. In Milan, I surrounded myself with the wrong people while I was with Loredana. The same thing happened in Los Angeles with Kari. I suppose it all came down to my fear of conflict. I was, and still am, terrified of confrontation. I'd rather retreat than stand up and fight for something.

Kari and I stayed together, but we also spent a lot of time apart, which, in my mind, was better than breaking up. We never talked about having kids. It was out of the question for me. Both our lives were all over the place, travelling constantly, and children just didn't fit into that. I already had Robin, and even being present for him was hard enough. Neither of us had any desire to get married either. After two failed marriages, I felt that what we had was good enough as it was.

The family house in Cap Ferrat had been sold too, one of the few places, along with Kättilö, that really meant something to me. Instead, I bought an apartment on Strandvägen in Stockholm, and Kari helped decorate it. Aside from dreaming of a career in Hollywood, she also wanted to be an interior designer, so I gave her free rein. Strandvägen is one of the fanciest addresses in Stockholm, and once again I don't know what I was thinking, because I never felt at home there either.

After the collapse in Holland, it took a while before I played another tournament. But eventually, life on the senior tour rolled on, and I faced my friend Vitas many times. I never enjoyed playing matches against him, it felt strange to train together and then compete as opponents.

In September 1994, Vitas and I were at a senior tournament in Seattle with Jimmy Connors and many others. One evening we played doubles, Vitas and I on opposite sides of the net again. John Lloyd and I played against Vitas and Jimmy, and we won. Normally we would have celebrated after a match, but not this time.

Vitas had always been a party guy, but in recent years, he'd turned his life around and become a clean-living person.

The very next day, Vitas flew back to New York to lead a couple of tennis clinics for sponsors. At that time, he was living in a guesthouse-poolhouse combo at the home of Marty Raynes, one of the wealthiest men in New York and a total tennis fanatic. Vitas moved easily in those circles, just as comfortable among billionaires as in more modest settings. Even Donald Trump was someone both Vitas and I bumped into now and then, as he liked tennis and sometimes came to watch us play in New York. Still, Vitas never forgot his humble beginnings. His family had fled Lithuania during the early days of the Second World War, when things were turning dangerous. They had been fairly well-off there, but his father Vytautas and mother Aldona left for an uncertain life in Brooklyn. Their family bond was incredibly strong, they all lived together in the same house on Long Island.

Once, Vitas and I travelled to his 'other homeland', Lithuania, to play an exhibition match in front of excited fans. Vitas and Lithuania were a golden combination. No one cared about me there, they were all there for him, and I thought it was wonderful. It turned out to be his first and only trip to the country.

Two days after Vitas left us in Seattle, we got the devastating phone call. None of us could believe it, it was such a shock. Vitas had died in a tragic accident. We simply couldn't grasp it. He had just been with us, playing, laughing, full of life, just like always.

At the time of the accident, he was staying at the Raynes family home. He had gone into the poolhouse to lie down and rest. When he didn't come out, they got worried and went in. That's where they found him, lying there lifeless. A faulty ventilation unit had leaked gas, which rendered him unconscious and then killed him. We were told he hadn't felt a thing. A small comfort, maybe. All of us who were still in Seattle cried together.

The tour schedule said we were supposed to continue on to Mexico City for more matches, and despite the heartbreak, we chose to go through with it. After the tournament, Jimmy Connors, Guillermo Vilas and I decided to take Jimmy's private jet to New York to attend the funeral on Long Island, while

Kari stayed behind in Mexico City to handle the luggage and logistics. We had to refuel in Houston, so we stayed on board. When border officials came in, they noticed I didn't have a visa to stay in the US, but they were kind and let it slide. Eventually, we landed at a small airport on Long Island. Thankfully, they didn't check there, and we made it to the church with just thirty minutes to spare. John McEnroe was already there, along with many friends and members of Vitas's family.

John, Jimmy, Guillermo and I carried Vitas's casket out of the church and into the waiting hearse. We were all deeply affected by his sudden passing and the tragedy of it all. We had lost a close friend, and it was heartbreaking to see his mother, father and sister so devastated. Vitas had never married and had no children, and I think that was a real sorrow for him. Maybe that's why he formed such a strong bond with Robin, as if Robin were the son he never had.

I still miss him every day and wish with all my heart that he had lived longer than those far too few forty years. But I have a strong sense that he's still with me, watching over me, and that he sees I'm finally happy.

I had lost Vitas, but during those years, I found two new friends who would come to mean a great deal to me: Johan Eliasch and Anders Wiklöf. I'm not someone with a lot of friends, but these two have become important to me, and they're still in my life today. I trust them completely, which is rare for me after everything I've been through.

Anders lives in Åland, an archipelago of Swedish-speaking islands located between Sweden and Finland that belonged to the latter. He's a real entrepreneur, incredibly proactive. He introduced senior tennis tournaments there and brought many of my old tennis buddies over. Thanks to his initiative, I've often gone over to visit. Sometimes he would call and say, 'Björn, how are you doing?' in his calm, distinctive Åland dialect. If I had a few free days, I'd happily head to Anders and his wife Rita in the beautiful Åland archipelago. He even sent a helicopter for me once, or sometimes his private plane. Åland has always felt like a safe haven. With Anders, I can be myself. We talk about everything, from serious topics to the lightest of things. He was also close to my parents while they were alive. If he couldn't reach me, he'd call my mum just to check on all of us. Our families share a strong bond. Anders and Rita never miss a birthday or forget to send Christmas flowers.

Johan Eliasch is my other close friend, and like Anders, he's an entrepreneur through and through. Johan is the CEO of the tennis brand Head, my main sponsor during the senior tour. We're similar in many ways, and nowadays, we enjoy spending time together with our families. He doesn't have many close friends either, and like me, he hates being alone. He'll call and say he wants me to come down to Saint-Tropez just to hang out.

From the moment Johan and I met, we've been close. We're both spontaneous – when we want to see each other, we just make it happen. And it helps that he has his own plane that can pick us up wherever we are. He even comes to the airport in his helicopter, which he keeps in his backyard and pilots himself. That's how it's always been with me. If something isn't smooth and simple, it doesn't happen.

We first met in the early '90s at Lake Como. Head was holding an event, and I was there as one of the senior players they sponsored. Johan had bought the company from the Austrian government when it was on the verge of bankruptcy and later managed to turn it around. Today, it's one of the most popular brands in tennis, and huge in alpine skiing too. Alpine skiing is one of Johan's big passions, and we've gone on many ski trips together. He's quite adventurous, and sometimes he's roped me into things that seem completely insane in hindsight, especially when you think about what happened to Michael Schumacher.

Once, in Kitzbühel, Austria, we took the lift up to the start gate of the Hahnenkamm downhill race, one of the most dangerous slopes in the world. It was Johan, me and skiing legend Franz Klammer. I was definitely the amateur of the group, but we got it in our heads that we should try skiing part of the course. I was terrified and should've stayed at the top, but my male pride wouldn't let me. I had to do it. Somehow, I made it down, although I don't know how, it feels like I had my eyes closed half the way.

Like Franz Klammer, Johan knows a ton of famous people – Formula 1 drivers, politicians, you name it. In that way, he reminds me of Vitas, with his huge network of interesting people. No matter where we were in the world, we always ended up invited to something. And I'd be the quiet guy tagging along.

Johan and I meet up as often as we can. He's always busy, always in different time zones, but we make it work. We always played doubles together in the pro/am tournaments in the Hamptons and in Saint-Tropez, where a professional is paired with an amateur. In winter, we often went to Phuket, Thailand, to a place called Amanpuri. Back in the '90s, it was the hotspot, everyone wanted to go there, and there were parties in every villa. We'd play tennis and work out during the day, though not always seriously. Johan likes to remind me how I once ran on the treadmill faster than him while holding a beer in my hand.

Johan's house in Thailand was always lively. Belinda Carlisle from the Go-Gos and her husband, Morgan Mason, were often there too, and we spent a lot of time together, both there and in LA. Morgan was a jack-of-all-trades, best known as an actor but also involved in politics, which sparked some heated but fascinating conversations. The house next door was owned by fashion designer Kenzo, and his place was always free access, kind of like an open house for everyone looking to party. It was easy to get to know everyone and it felt like one big, shared vacation.

By the late 1990s, I was still emotionally unsettled. I was tired of my strange relationship with Kari, which never seemed to go anywhere, and I was looking for something more: real love, stability, a true home. I even thought about whether one of my exes might have been 'the one' all along, and whether I had made a mistake by letting them go.

So one time I took Jannike and Robin with me on one of my trips to Thailand. I wanted to kill two birds with one stone: spend more time with Robin and see where things stood between me and Jannike. I did something similar with Helena Anliot. Deep down, I knew our relationship was long over, but I still sought her out again just to see if any spark remained. Just two days after landing back in Stockholm with Jannike and Robin, I hopped on a flight to Australia, where Helena lived. It was nice to see her again, we had a lot to talk about, but deep down, I knew we didn't have what it took to start over.

Back at square one, I decided to give happiness another shot. Kari was still in the picture in some way. We'd never truly broken things off, and I was ready to give it one last try. I boarded a flight to Los Angeles. During a layover in Chicago, I called Kari and told her I was on my way. She replied that she had gone to Hawaii. Still, she said I could stay at the apartment in LA and wait for her to come back in four days. That was all the confirmation I needed for what I'd already felt inside.

I'd had enough. It was time to stop all the indecision and back-and-forth. I changed my booking and took the first flight back to Stockholm. There was a woman there I knew I liked, someone who just might be exactly what I was looking for: Patricia Östfeldt.

It was worth a serious try, finally building the life I truly wanted.

PART FIVE

Game, Set, Match (2000–2025)

28

True Love

The first time Patricia and I had crossed paths was a year and a half earlier, when she was sitting in the front row watching one of my matches. We didn't meet that time, but her interest in tennis meant that, thanks to fate – or maybe some higher power – we heard about each other not long afterwards.

Patricia had gone on a promotional trip to the Canary Islands with Björn Borg Underwear, together with her friend Wania, who ran a clothing boutique in Stockholm. The trip included a bit of tennis, and when Patricia ran into my friend Anders Rosén, both he and others, funnily enough, started talking about how perfect we would be for each other. Even though neither of us was looking for anyone at the moment, the talk had made me curious.

To my delight, Patricia started playing more tennis after the trip and joined a tennis club just outside Stockholm, where she trained with Anders. I played there too, and soon we started running into each other from time to time. All the training sessions began with coffee in the reception area, and we'd chat whenever we got the chance. It was ideal for me, tennis halls weren't as awkward as bars could be, and we had a chance to get a sense of each other. I started to grow interested in her.

One day, during one of those sessions, Joakim Nyström, one of Sweden's top players, showed up and asked if we'd play an exhibition match in his home town, Skellefteå. It was for a good cause, and I usually say yes to that sort of thing. Anders and I talked about it at the club, and Patricia and Wania overheard and got really excited. They decided right away to go and watch the match. Anders and I were going to fly up with his dad, who had a pilot's licence and flew both passengers and cargo. Patricia and Wania flew up a day or two later.

That was the start, tentative and nervous, of our love story. We met after the match at dinner, and Patricia was really impressed because she thought I was drinking milk when it was actually a White Russian. We barely slept that night.

Wania had an important meeting the next day and wanted to get home as quickly as possible, but I wasn't quite ready to let Patricia go. I still had a bit of clout at the time, so I simply called the airport and asked them to hold the flight, which they did. Naturally, the other passengers weren't thrilled. When it turned out the delay was due to two slightly tired girls heading home, the business travellers weren't exactly pleased.

When we were back in Stockholm, I asked Patricia if she wanted to play tennis with me, and that's how we kept seeing each other. As Easter approached, she gave me an Easter egg with her favourite perfume inside, so I could smell her whenever I wanted. I have to admit, I thought that was really sweet. I was falling for her more and more, even though I was still scarred from past relationships and hadn't completely let go of Kari.

Eventually, after circling around each other for a while, we decided to go on our first real, serious date, at Edsbacka Krog, a restaurant outside Stockholm with two Michelin stars. If I hadn't felt like I had something big to lose, the date might've been easy. After all, we'd seen each other a bunch of times. But this was different. I don't think I've ever been so nervous in my life. So much was riding on it. I knew Patricia was smart, and I kept thinking, what do I even have to offer? What if I just sat there silently the whole dinner? But I'd also made up my mind: I wasn't going to let this woman go.

I picked her up in a taxi, and if I'd been nervous before, it was nothing compared to now. I was sweating like crazy in my winter coat – why I was wearing it in spring, I have no idea. A Wimbledon final had nothing on this. It felt like the match of my life, and I already knew in the taxi it was going to go to five sets. How would I entertain this woman for that long? Keep a conversation going? I'm such a closed-off person.

We survived the taxi ride, and once we walked into Edsbacka Krog, I felt like I'd won the first game. The restaurant was a converted seventeenth-century inn with lots of small rooms, not a big, crowded dining hall, which was a relief. Still, things could easily go wrong. Would I try a bad joke that neither of us got? Would I mess everything up again?

But once we sat down, something happened. Of course, Patricia could tell how nervous I was and, with ease, took charge of the situation. She must've looked at me and thought: this guy needs help. Suddenly everything just flowed. It was magical. Patricia was generous and carried the conversation, and I could just go along. After a little while, I even started opening up to her, it was obvious. It felt so easy, like running water. She had that gift. I told her things about myself that I'd never told any woman before. We talked about funny stuff and serious topics, loneliness, past relationships.

The only thing that threw me a little was when Patricia stepped away with the waiter to admire the view. I got jealous. I can get so incredibly jealous, especially when I have something to lose. She probably picked up on that too and maybe thought I deserved to squirm a bit. But once she came back, I forgot all about it and just enjoyed being with her.

Not long after the date, it was time for the annual Monte Carlo tournament. I wasn't playing, but I wanted to go because Labbe was to be honoured with a prize there. I found out Patricia would be going too, it was her thirtieth birthday present. I went down a few days before her, but told her to let me know when she arrived.

As I always did while competing, I stayed at Hôtel Hermitage. Labbe and his wife, Rose-Marie, 'Munda', were there too. The same night Patricia was arriving, we were celebrating Labbe. Once the party was over, I continued on my own. When Patricia got to the hotel and asked for me, the staff told her to wait in the lobby while they tried to locate me. They gave her some sweets and a drink, probably thinking it was a bit rude I wasn't around. But in Monte Carlo, everyone always knows where everyone is. The city's not that big, and it didn't take long for them to find me at the casino.

I wasn't exactly eager to leave the table, I felt like luck was on my side and didn't want to walk away. Maybe I was also confused about everything. Sure, Patricia and I had had a great date, but Kari was still haunting me. Eventually, I realised Patricia must be worried, so I went back to the hotel. It was wonderful to see her, and we went out for dinner. We ended up staying up all night.

The next morning, I was flying back to Sweden with Labbe, while Patricia stayed for the finals. We were both exhausted after that night, but it didn't matter.

*

Once I was back home, I decided to go to Los Angeles to see Kari. I needed to know if there was anything left between us. It was like I had two relationships happening at the same time. All I knew for sure was that I couldn't handle being alone. And things with Patricia weren't exactly simple either. She had a job, a great apartment, two small kids – she had a lot to lose, and being with someone like me seemed risky. Patricia knew about my other relationship, and that it was messy. She probably wasn't thrilled, but she accepted it, and I had made up my mind to go.

So I got on a plane to LA, with a stopover in Chicago. When I called Kari and found out she was in Hawaii, the truth hit me. All the back-and-forth with Kari, all the hard decisions I never made, all the conflicts I was scared of. That was it. I changed all my bookings and headed home. I finally had my exit.

On the flight back, I just felt huge relief. I knew there was a woman waiting for me, and now I could finally focus on that and leave all the craziness behind. Somewhere over the Atlantic, I made up my mind, I wasn't letting go again.

It felt like the flight flew by. I was in a daze and went straight from the airport to the tennis hall in Sundbyberg, where I figured Patricia might be. Sure enough, I saw her from the car, standing with her kids and Wania. I got out and walked straight up to her. She looked completely stunned.

'But . . . You're supposed to be in LA!'

'Not any more. I turned around in Chicago.'

Then we stood there, hugging, and I guess you could say that's when we officially became a couple, fittingly, outside a tennis club in Sundbyberg. I'd made up my mind, and thankfully, so had she. This woman was different from anyone I'd ever been with before.

Confident that she was the one, I wanted to tell Patricia's ex-husband, Patrik, the father of her kids, as soon as possible.

I wanted Patricia to know I was serious, and I wanted to prove to both her and myself that I could take responsibility. This was totally new for me, but I figured it was best to get it over with. So we went straight to Patrik's apartment. I thought I needed to speak to him alone, so Patricia waited in the car. Without ever having met him, I knocked on the door and asked to talk.

'I've made up my mind about Patricia,' I said.

Patrik didn't look convinced, he just stared at me.

'I'll take care of the kids and everything too,' I added.

'Yeah, sure,' he said. Of course he didn't believe a word I said. He probably had his own ideas about me from what he'd read in the papers. But he had no choice but to accept it, even if he didn't like it. This time, I wanted to do things right and take care of everyone involved. Today, many years later, Patrik and I can actually laugh about that day, which was a pretty strange one. 'You stole my wife,' he likes to joke.

Patricia was waiting anxiously in the car, wondering what I'd said and how Patrik had reacted. But that was something between me and Patrik. I just told her, 'It's all good.'

Patricia and I were so in love with each other, and after every dinner that turned into an evening at my place on Strandvägen, I always hated it when she had to leave. I'd try to make her stay as long as possible. I often asked if we could watch a movie, like *Gladiator*. It's one of my favourites, and also one of the longest. We watched it several times just to stretch out the night. Sometimes, when she had to go, we'd watch it on fast-forward, just so she'd stay a little longer.

Every time she said, 'I have to go,' it stung. The loneliness hit hard. Even though I knew Patricia and I were together now, that fear of being alone still crept in. I was so used to being the centre of attention and having someone look after me, ever since I was a kid. If no one was watching, I could mess things up in all kinds of ways. Patricia gave me that sense of care, and incredibly, she still had her own life, her own interests, a strong will, and a career as a real estate agent.

It wasn't long before we took our relationship more seriously and Patricia moved in with me on Strandvägen. 'Well that didn't take long,' some people said. It depends on who you ask. I thought those two months felt like for ever, but for Patricia, it was fast.

From then on, we were inseparable. I wanted to show her everything about me, and I wanted to start right away. We booked our first trip together, to Marbella, where my friend Manolo Santana was hosting an exhibition tournament. Outwardly, Patricia and I kept a low profile. I was still fair game for the world press. In Marbella, I even arranged for us to stay in separate hotel rooms to throw people off. Of course, Patricia only used hers when she needed to grab clothes and change. The whole trip was amazing and we had a great time. My friends at the exhibition had seen me with other women before, but now they could tell it was serious. I was calmer, more grounded, physically and mentally.

We'd barely made it home from Marbella when Johan Eliasch called and asked me to come to Saint-Tropez. I asked Patricia to come too. I wanted her to meet Johan, who meant a lot to me. She was hesitant at first, so I went to the airport alone. But I left a ticket at the airline office that could be used at any point, in case she changed her mind. I hadn't even boarded before she caught up and came with me.

That second trip was just as lovely. We had wonderful days on the French Riviera, and I don't think Patricia regretted coming. The only downside was the constant paparazzi lurking in every corner. A few times we had to duck into hotels and restaurants to hide. There wasn't anything secret going on, but I wanted to protect my new private life.

I also wanted Patricia to meet my friend Anders Wiklöf, so when he hosted his annual senior tournament in Åland later that summer, I asked if she would like to come. Luckily, she did, and it was especially fun since I was defending my title from the year before. Those tournaments don't leave much free time, but I brought Robin too. It was the first time Patricia and he had been in the same place, and I was so happy to see them together. It made our relationship feel even more real, even if they were both a little shy.

The weekend flew by. I played well and made it to the final, though I lost. But it didn't matter. That incredible summer, in a very short time, Patricia had met the most important people in my life.

Despite all the travel, the summer felt long, and we spent lots of time out at Alstaholm with my parents. Patricia's children, Kasper and Bianca, came along too. We all stayed in the little guest wing next to the main house. It was so nice to get out of the city and be near the water and that feeling of freedom. We went out with the boat often, got to know each other on a deeper level, kids and adults alike, and stayed close the whole time.

That was something new for me. I was really going all in on family life, trying to learn how to be a good role model and a friend Patricia's kids could count on. Spending that much time with Patricia out at Alstaholm changed something in me. For the first time, I felt truly at home. It didn't matter that we were cramped and right next to my parents, I was happy.

All I needed was a small guest wing, and Patricia.

29

The Weddings

I knew right away that I wanted to marry Patricia, even though my two previous marriages hadn't ended well. I remember thinking about what I could do differently this time, but honestly, I had no idea. I just knew I had to hold on. I stuck to the promise I'd made to myself: this was too good, I couldn't let her go.

In September 2001, I got down on one knee. It was at a hotel in Corsica. Everything was perfect, the sun was shining, the view of the Mediterranean was magical. As I knelt in front of Patricia, there was a long, drawn-out second of silence. She didn't say anything, I could tell she was giggling to herself. But after she got over the internal laughter at the fact that I was actually kneeling in front of her, she said yes.

It was one of the happiest moments of my life.

When we got home, the wedding planning began. We had set the date for 8 June 2002, at Ingarö church out in the Stockholm archipelago. Unlike my previous weddings, I was much more involved in the planning this time. Helping us was Alexandra Charles, whom I'd known for years. We had countless meetings in our kitchen, going over everything down to the smallest detail. Alexandra is known for leaving nothing to chance, and this time was no different. I trusted her completely, she'd always looked out for me over the years. If I was at Alexandra's club, she always made sure I had a good table. If I wanted privacy, I got it. If I wanted company, which I usually did, she could quickly put together a perfect group with compatible interests.

I had no idea how much work a wedding actually required. We had to talk to the pastor and all sorts of other people involved. Patricia was in contact with the opera singer Anne Sofie von Otter, whom the Swedish king had honoured as a Court Singer and who would sing at the church. I arranged for Loa Falkman, another Court Singer, to perform as well.

At the same time, I was still playing tennis and training as much as I could, as much as my body would allow. By then, I could tell my body was a bit worn out after so many years of intense training, but I played a few exhibition tournaments and was still competing on the senior tour.

We decided to take a little vacation over Christmas and New Year. We went to Barbados and a charming hotel called Sandy Lane where I'd been a few years earlier and knew some people. Maybe that was partly because Alexandra Charles had been married to a man from Barbados and even ran a sister club to Alexandra's on the island. Sandy Lane has fantastic tennis facilities, so the vacation pretty much turned into a boot camp. We played every morning, and in the afternoons we rented jet skis and cruised around the island. Patricia got so sore from the workouts that she had to walk backwards down the hotel stairs.

She played her best tennis ever there at Sandy Lane, after

training quite a bit with Percy Rosberg. She's a fierce competitor and has a fiery temper, which don't always go well together. Deep down she knew she'd never beat me, but once she was on the court, she thought she was Serena Williams. At one point she completely lost it and smashed all her rackets after losing a point. That was the end of tennis for that trip, since the capital, Bridgetown, didn't exactly have a great selection of new rackets. Luckily, there were only a few days left of the vacation, and we finally got to relax.

Back home, the wedding preparations continued. The reception was going to be at Wermdö Golf Club, a place I'd always been fond of. We'd often gone there by boat, especially back in the days when they had their legendary Wednesday night discos that all of Stockholm flocked to. Boats would be docked all over the bay, and on Thursday mornings champagne bottles floated in the water and partygoers lay asleep on the beach. It's a beautiful lakeside spot and perfect for a June wedding.

Then there was the matter of the first dance. Sure, dancing at Studio 54 might've been fun, but otherwise my memories of the Wimbledon balls were mostly dreadful. Now I had to practise for our wedding waltz every week. It didn't go well. Not even Patricia thought it was fun. We both have two left feet when it comes to dancing.

In the middle of all the planning, it was time for the bachelor and bachelorette parties. Somehow, we managed to have them at the same time, because Patricia and I didn't want to be apart more than absolutely necessary.

Patricia had a lovely, cosy weekend with friends and a spa retreat. My friend Johan Eliasch organised my bachelor party, and that turned into something else entirely. The plans were grand, I knew about them from the start. My dad, Labbe, Johan and I were going to fly around the world in his private plane. First stop Moscow. Then on to Phuket in Thailand, where we always spent Christmas and New Year together. The idea was that each stop would be unique and exciting, with a vibrant nightlife. After Phuket: Los Angeles, Paris, and back to Stockholm. I was really looking forward to a couple of great weeks with my core crew.

But that's not how it turned out. Instead of leaving from Arlanda, we were picked up at Bromma Airport just outside Stockholm and flown directly to Paris, our final destination. None of us really knew why the plans had changed, but we didn't mind too much. We were just happy to be together, and we figured Johan had something fun up his sleeve.

We arrived at the hotel in Paris and unpacked. Then Johan said he and I should head over to an apartment to prep for the evening's dinner. When we got there, a strange woman was already there, and I immediately felt something was off. What did she have to do with my bachelor party? She would be joining us for dinner, as would some of her friends. I instantly realised this whole setup was just an excuse for Johan to spend time with her, and I felt pretty cheated out of my bachelor party before it had even started.

I went back to the hotel and had a drink with Labbe and my dad. We decided it didn't really matter, we had our little gang, and we always had a great time together. Of course we considered skipping Johan's 'date night', as we now called the dinner, but I had promised to go.

After dinner, we all went out to explore the Paris nightlife, including my dad and Labbe. Nothing strange about that, they always stayed out until the very end. Johan knew the Paris scene and got us into the VIP section of an exclusive nightclub. We had barely sat down when I heard someone shout, 'Hey Björn, old friend! Come have a drink!' I turned around, and there was Ron Wood from the Rolling Stones. It was such a joy to see Ronnie again. We've met many times over the years, and whenever we do, it's like no time has passed, we just pick up where we left off.

In the end, the bachelor party wasn't much of a bachelor party, and sure, I was a bit disappointed at the time. But looking back, I couldn't have asked for more. I ran into Ronnie and had a great weekend with my dad and Labbe. Even today, Johan and I still laugh about that so-called bachelor party.

At last 8 June arrived. Patricia had chosen a dress designed for her by Lars Wallin, who had spent countless hours creating a stunning gown made of silk, lace and pearls. We all stood there in the blazing heat, waiting to see her. One hundred and thirty guests had come from all over the world, many visiting Sweden for the first time. Everyone was surprised at how warm it was in 'cold' Sweden.

Patricia arrived by water in a beautiful mahogany boat with her father and Wania, her maid of honour. We guys – me, my dad and Robin – had already arrived in a cool limousine. But the boat ride took longer than expected, they were enjoying themselves and didn't hurry. I actually started to worry that she'd changed her mind.

But of course, they arrived eventually, and once we'd said our vows and the ceremony was over, we finally got to greet all our guests. It felt like everyone was genuinely happy for us. Patricia and I took the same boat to Wermdö Golf Club, where the reception was held. The boat was stunning, a classic luxury yacht built in 1913 for Ivar Kreuger, the Swedish financier. It had carried many famous passengers, including Greta Garbo and Douglas Fairbanks. It was one of the best days of my life, having all my friends there and finally marrying the love of my life. I kept thinking about the promise I'd made to myself: to do everything I could to make this last for ever.

We ate an incredible meal, laughed and cried through all the speeches, and then came the wedding waltz. You'd never have guessed how much we'd practised, but it didn't matter. The guests joined in and danced along. I especially remember Grandma Greta, how quickly she hit the dance floor. We had lost Grandpa a year earlier, for the second time really, since he had suffered from dementia in his final years. Grandma enjoyed every moment of that day, barefoot, like the wonderful original she was. Everyone wanted to dance with her. Over ninety and so full of life! She and Patricia got along so well, they'd often sit in her wing of the house out in the country, talking about life. She was happy I'd met a 'normal' girl.

The guest list was a colourful mix. In addition to family and friends, most of Sweden's tennis elite were there, along with Ilie Năstase, Guillermo Vilas and Mansour Bahrami and their spouses. The only people I really missed were a few international tennis friends who were playing the French Open at the time.

As tradition has it, the bride and groom are supposed to leave the party first, but we had mixed feelings about it. We would've loved to stay and chat with everyone, but it had already been a long day. We were staying at the Grand Hotel in Saltsjöbaden, which is also in the Stockholm archipelago.

When we finally made it up to the suite – a turret room with a view of the water – we were both hungry and thirsty, but everything was closed and there was nothing in the room. That was a bit of a letdown. All we wanted was to get home, eat, drink and be with our family.

The room was so hot all night that we couldn't take it any more. Early in the morning, we hopped in a taxi and went straight to Alstaholm. When we arrived at dawn, the family had already kicked off the day with champagne and breakfast. Everyone was surprised to see us back so soon. There they were, laughing, talking and having a great time. We felt a bit like we'd missed out, but now the celebration could continue.

The summer was beautiful, and we decided to stay in Sweden and save our honeymoon for September when the heat would ease up. So that summer we took the boat out to sea and were away as much as possible. After a night in Västervik, we decided to cross over to Gotland, an island off the coast of Sweden, once a medieval stronghold and now also a popular summer destination. We were in a fairly small boat without GPS, but we had a compass and it was enough to navigate since Gotland is directly east of Västervik. Our phones quickly lost signal once we were out in open water, but all was well. The sun was shining.

A bit later, though it was still sunny, a sudden storm rolled in out of nowhere. Winds like hell itself. The waves grew so big that we disappeared in them, and the boat started filling with water at an alarming rate. We had thankfully brought extra fuel in case the tank didn't last the whole way, and it was a good thing we did, because there was no way we could've refuelled in those winds. We couldn't follow the compass any more and were forced to focus solely on riding out the waves. We didn't see a single boat, everyone else had probably listened to the weather warnings. I got genuinely scared. I honestly thought we might not make it. The only thing I could hear, or felt I could hear, was my own heartbeat. Patricia tried talking to me, but I couldn't respond. I had to focus on every single wave and how to negotiate it.

After more than six hours, we finally saw land behind us. We'd missed Gotland and were headed into the open Baltic. Luckily, we'd caught a glimpse of the island and were able to turn around and make it ashore. Because of the storm, there were hardly any boats in the harbour. The harbour master assumed we were arriving with a boat that belonged to a larger ship out at sea. When we told them we'd come all the way from Västervik, no one believed us.

After that trip, we always stayed close to land, and we never tried sailing to Gotland again.

At the end of the summer, Patricia started feeling nauseous and tired all the time. She took a pregnancy test – it was positive. That was the beginning of Leo's journey.

We had talked early on about wanting a child together, and we decided that if it happened, it happened. We didn't have to wait long, and we were so grateful. One of the first people to find out was Grandma Greta. She was over the moon and toasted with her whisky and pipe another great-grandchild to love! Sadly, she didn't get to meet Leo – she passed away that autumn. She stayed sharp until the very end. On the day she died, she had even been to IKEA to buy new furniture. Who does that at over ninety?

The idea of a September honeymoon had seemed great at first, but travelling that far while pregnant turned out to be no picnic. We were hesitant, but in the end, we went to Bora Bora near Tahiti. Neither of us had been there, and we wanted to experience the islands. After a journey of nearly forty-eight hours, we arrived. Patricia had felt sick the whole flight and tried to sleep through it. I watched movies – it felt like we'd never get there.

Once we arrived, we stayed in a classic island bungalow, built on stilts above the water, with glass floors so you could watch the fish swim below. When we checked in, we gave our address as Monte Carlo. The concierge looked up and asked, 'What are you doing here if you could be in Monte Carlo?' We kind of wondered the same, but we wanted to make the most of it and just enjoy ourselves. We spent our days in the sun and the water – when Patricia wasn't napping, that is. There were no TV channels except Bloomberg, which only showed stock prices. There was a twelve-hour time difference, and since Patricia was still working, she had to wake up early to reach all the real estate buyers and sellers back home.

On top of that, the paparazzi had found us. The island had just one hotel, so we were easy to track down. They sat in the trees and bushes around the property.

After a couple of weeks, we'd had enough of Bloomberg and naps. It was time to go home.

In October 2016, it happened again. I'd reached my goal: Patricia and I were still happily married. But I felt like I wanted to propose all over again, to strengthen our bond even more. This time, I wanted something more spontaneous, no bachelor party, no big to-do.

We travelled to the west coast of the US. Patricia had never been there before, and I wanted to show her Los Angeles, where I'd once lived on and off. It felt important for her to know about that part of my life, even if she hadn't been there back then. We visited Malibu, Santa Monica and Venice Beach. We also planned to fly to Las Vegas for a few nights, I wanted to show her that too.

We stayed in a quieter part of Caesar's Palace called Nobu. Unfortunately, the hotel sponsorship was no longer in place, so we had to book and pay for everything ourselves this time. When we got to our room, the champagne was chilling. Once again, I got down on one knee, for the second time, to the same wife.

'Will you marry me?'

Even though we were already married, I was nervous and sweating. Patricia just laughed, but for the second time, she said yes.

Unfortunately, I'm terrible at planning and organising, so she had to arrange the rest. I'd heard about an Elvis impersonator who had married other tennis guys, including Andre Agassi. Patricia tracked him down and booked a time. Elvis Presley had always been special to me. It started when I was a kid, when we often played his songs in Labbe's VW bus. I was lucky enough to see him live once, in Hawaii in 1973. It was unforgettable. He was still in great shape and sang beautifully. Now it felt right to honour my old idol by having the wedding in his spirit.

We bought new clothes, and the excitement was just as real as when we'd got married at Ingarö church fourteen years earlier. Everything was meticulously arranged. There were two wedding witnesses, it wasn't some quick drive-through ceremony like you might think. We got to choose which Elvis songs would play during the ceremony, and we renewed our vows to each other. Elvis himself even gave us an extra song as a gift – he'd noticed Patricia's shoes, which were, of course, Blue Suede Shoes. Fitting! Afterwards, we called my mum and Patricia's parents. They congratulated us again, and the only thing they said was they wished they could've been there.

It was 30 October. Now we have two anniversaries to celebrate.

30

'We've Reached the Bottom'

I n 2000, I was named 'Swedish Athlete of the Century' at
Sweden's big Sports Gala. It was about time Sweden organised
a proper event to honour all our amazing athletes – other countries had been doing it for years. The competition was tough,
and in the end, it came down to me and Ingemar Stenmark,
the legendary alpine skier, who had done an incredible amount
for Swedish sport. Our king, Carl XVI Gustaf, presented the
award, and today the statue has a place of honour in my home.
It's one of the heaviest trophies I have, not just in terms of
weight, but in meaning. It was the Swedish people who voted
for me, and that means a lot.

Joining me at the gala to receive the award were Labbe
and Kari (this was before I'd met Patricia). It meant a lot to
have Labbe there, because I could never thank him enough
for everything he had done for me. The moment I was named
Athlete of the Century was incredibly emotional for both of us.
Through all the years, even during my time on the senior tour,

he'd looked after me, mentally and physically. He was such a big part of my entire career and was constantly by my side. He was like a second father to me. The downside was that he was always away from his own family, and I often felt guilty about getting more of his time than his own kids did. Really, they should've been at the gala too.

Once I started playing on the senior tour, Labbe and I mostly saw each other when I came back to Sweden. I'd call him the moment I landed. I wanted to talk to him, and get one of his famously tough massages. He never stopped giving those.

Our families were also close. Labbe's wife, Munda, often came along to the bigger tournaments I played. We usually spent holidays like Christmas, Easter, Midsummer and crayfish season together. Midsummer was probably the most popular. We'd start with a light lunch, then decorate the maypole, followed by the traditional dancing. Thankfully, we knew a lot of musicians, so there was always someone to provide music. After dinner, no one ever wanted to leave, and the evenings ended late. I used to call them 'twelve-hour lunches'. They started at noon and – on a good day! – wrapped up just after midnight. Sometimes we hosted the parties at Kättilö or Alstaholm in Sweden, and when my parents had their house in Cap Ferrat, Labbe would bring the whole wonderful family down there. Munda had a great sense of humour, and Labbe and I loved to tease her. One time we threw her in the pool – not our best prank, since she was fully dressed and had spent hours on her hair and makeup for the evening's festivities.

Our friendship lasted through the years, and when Patricia and I had our son Leo, it was obvious that Labbe would be his godfather. He didn't have any grandchildren of his own yet, so it felt good to give something back in that way.

It also gave us another reason to meet up. In addition to

holidays, we had a tradition where, once a year, Dad, Labbe and I would take the boat out. The destination varied, but often it was Sandhamn, and we'd be out all day, from early morning to late evening. We made sure to stock up on good food and drinks, and once out on the water, we were in our element. We all loved that sense of freedom and made up a golden trio, just like when Dad and I used to travel to Antibes and Saint-Tropez years earlier.

Our conversations were always about shared memories. We'd been through so much fun and madness, there was never a shortage of things to talk about. We loved joking around, but we never talked about life in the present. That was a clear boundary.

By the time we got home, we were usually far from sober, let's put it that way. Patricia, Munda and my mum Margareta would often watch us trying to dock the boat. 'Who's going to fall in this time?' was their favourite guessing game. Usually it was Labbe. Even though they were both a lot older than me, Labbe and my dad were my closest friends, and we kept that boat tradition going year after year. It was a wonderful time, one you thought would never end.

But unfortunately, it did. Everything ends. In 2008, Labbe was admitted to Huddinge Hospital. I didn't realise how ill he was at the time and carried on planning a trip to Shanghai, where I was supposed to work an event for Rolex. Then one night, the phone rang, and I got the devastating news that Labbe was no longer with us. It had happened incredibly fast; he'd become seriously ill in such a short time. I remember dropping the phone onto the floor. The shock was overwhelming. When I lay down that night, and many nights afterwards, memories from our life together replayed in my mind over and over. I felt like I'd never find peace again. Labbe's death broke me for a long time. Or as Labbe himself would've said: 'We've reached the bottom.'

*

Even as grief hit me full force, I kept playing on the senior tour in the US and competed in a number of other tournaments and exhibitions around the world. I was basically active throughout the 2000s. The only real difference was that I was now based in Sweden, rather than Monte Carlo, Milan, Houston or Los Angeles. It was still lucrative to play, and I remained in high demand. But the older I got, the less seriously I took it all. Eventually, it became mostly exhibition matches where the games were for fun, and the payment came in the form of guaranteed fees – you got a set amount for showing up, regardless of whether you won. The competitive element had disappeared, and to be honest, sometimes we'd even decide beforehand who was going to win.

That kind of thing would've been unthinkable during my earlier years on the senior tour. Back then, it was all about winning, and there were intense negotiations about fees. For a long time, payment came in cash, at least at the exhibition events. I have no idea how it works today. When I was still playing ATP tournaments, we were always paid by wire transfer, but the sums were small. When I won Wimbledon in 1976 I think I only received 12,500 pounds. Compare that to today, when the winner gets 2.7 million. That's why, even back in 1979 or 1980, we started playing exhibitions: they were a good way to earn extra money. We even skipped some ATP tournaments because of them, which didn't go over well.

This eventually led to the agreement among us top players in Boca Raton. It was important to stay aligned with the group. We were all supposed to be equally absent. Whether it was a noble agreement or not is up for debate, but I was the only one who actually stuck to the deal.

The fact is, we players wanted it that way.

But it was a different time. Everything was paid in cash back then in the '90s. The downside was that huge sums of cash had to be transported all over the world. You were always a little nervous in certain countries, traveling with a tennis bag stuffed with bills. A lot could go wrong in those situations. There was always the risk of getting robbed, which actually did happen to me once, in Saint Petersburg, Russia.

I had just finished a senior event, and when we got to the airport to check in our bags, two of mine were missing. I needed them, so I went back to the hotel hoping they'd still be there. Sure enough, they were still in reception. But traffic back to the airport was chaos, and I realised I was going to miss my flight. I booked a new room and, feeling tired, stayed in, watched TV and ordered room service. Later that night, there was a knock at the door. Two guys were standing outside with a gun. They forced their way in and demanded all the money and valuables I had. I had no choice but to comply. It was probably an inside job, everything seemed too perfectly timed.

That was one of the times when my friend Anders Wiklöf sent his private plane to bring me home. I didn't feel right for a long time afterwards. The fear stuck with me.

Thankfully, that was the only time I was ever robbed. My biggest issue otherwise was always customs. It was always nerve-wracking getting through customs on the way home, often with more cash than was legally allowed. You never knew how customs officers would react. Would they be on your side or confiscate everything?

When I did get stopped, I had a go-to strategy: play dumb. 'Oh? Where did that money come from? Never seen it before.' Then you'd just have to bite the bullet and accept the loss. I don't know how many bags full of cash I've had taken – several, for sure. It was part of the game.

After a tournament in Italy, I was supposed to get $100,000.

It never showed up in my account, and I got no cash either. There was nothing I could do, we never signed contracts for obvious reasons. Another time, in the '90s, I won a lot of money in cash at a tournament in South America. I flew home to Sweden and got through customs fine. But when Jannike went to exchange some of it at the bank, it turned out the money was counterfeit. No point going back to complain.

One time, I got paid entirely in one-dollar bills and had to lug a giant Santa sack full of them through passport control. Customs officers must've laughed if they saw what I had. Another time, I and a few others wrapped up the US senior tour by travelling through Asia for some exhibition events. The final stop was India, and from there we would head to Paris, where we'd part ways. When I was packing, I realised I had to stuff all the cash into my racket bag and bring it as carry-on. The money took up so much space, there was no room for the rackets, so I left them in the hotel room.

When we arrived at the airport in Bombay, everyone else got through passport control quickly. In the end, it was just me and my friend Mansour Bahrami left. He stuck with me because he was sure I'd get caught for smuggling cash. Sure enough, a zealous customs officer saw the money-packed bag in the scanner, stopped me, and called over more officers. My legs were shaking, I felt sick with fear. The officer brought the bag to his superior and said: 'Look what I've found!'

The manager opened the bag, looked at the money, then at me. He looked very stern, zipped the bag shut again, and then broke into a smile: 'Have a nice flight, Mr Borg!'

I walked through on shaky legs, and Mansour was soaked in sweat from the stress. The customs officer looked crushed that he didn't get to bust me. That cash would be 'king' didn't mean much to me in that moment, I felt more like a criminal.

Mum was also used to handling large amounts of cash. She had some creative tactics. One of her most successful tricks was hiding bundles of bills inside a package of sanitary pads. When she did that, customs never stopped her. But sometimes, even she had trouble. On one occasion, customs in Nice called her to say her suitcase had been flagged and asked if she wanted to come and pick it up. It had sat unclaimed for a while. Of course, it was full of cash she'd planned to bring back to Sweden. She just ignored the call, scared as she was of getting in trouble for undeclared money. Customs kept the loot.

I used to give Grandma Greta some cash whenever I visited her in Fruängen. But she didn't trust it was safe to keep at home, so she carried it around in a sports bag. One day, she was going to visit my parents and packed the bag with around a million kronor, along with her whisky, pipe and cigarettes. When she remembered she'd forgotten something upstairs, she left the bag in the stairwell for a few minutes. Someone seized the opportunity and stole it. You can only imagine the thief's surprise when they opened it.

Whenever I got home to Sweden or Monte Carlo with a bag full of prize money, there was always the same routine. Whatever didn't stay stashed in the closet had to be exchanged into local currency. Each exchange office had a limit, so I'd have to drive around to a bunch of different ones to get it all changed.

This whole business of dealing with piles of cash went on for a long time, long enough that my son Leo experienced it too. I'll never forget what he once told his teacher on the first day of school. He was answering basic questions like where he lived, what his phone number was and what he wanted to be when he grew up. His answer came quickly: 'I live in a box, I have a secret number, and I have to exchange money.'

31

Family Life

I'm a family man. Once upon a time, it was just me and my parents. Now Patricia had turned that trio into a quartet. It was something new, but the bond was just as strong, and my mum and dad welcomed her as one of the family. Patricia has brought a lot to the table, and through her, we've managed to hold the family together despite all the challenges along the way.

Looking back, I think every member of my family has been a bit solitary and closed off in their own way. Patricia isn't like that, she has a rich social life and, thank God, she's great at keeping in touch with the people around us. That includes my old tennis buddies, who call her when they want to reach us. When we decide to throw a party, it's Patricia who makes sure it actually happens. I've never really managed to stay in touch with the people I've met over the years, famous or not. Musicians, athletes, businesspeople, I never kept any of their numbers in any organised way. All I had was an old-school phone book filled with scribbled-down numbers that were impossible to sort through. Patricia tried, but it was just a jumble of digits, no area codes, no country codes.

When we first met, I can't say her parents and friends were particularly thrilled. They were worried I wasn't serious enough about her, and of course, they only wanted what was best for her. That changed over time, and today I have a great relationship with everyone around her.

Leo was born in early summer 2003. Before he arrived, we spent a lot of time in Monte Carlo fixing up the apartment. We repainted, bought new furniture, did it all ourselves. We were thinking Leo might grow up and go to school there, but at the same time, we wanted him to be born in Sweden. So, in the final weeks before the birth, we spent a lot of time in front of the TV in our Strandvägen apartment. Mostly snooker, because the World Championship was on. I have to say, I'm really fascinated by that sport, and this time we got to watch every single match.

Leo was born on 15 May, the same day as Patricia's mother's birthday, so she got a pretty special gift that year. The birth went smoothly, but unfortunately, he developed colic almost immediately. Despite the joy, it was a tough time. He cried every day from afternoon until dawn, and it was heartbreaking not to be able to comfort him, to feel so helpless. We took turns sleeping and carrying him around. Then, almost like a miracle, three months later, he stopped crying and being in pain.

We spent most of Leo's first summer in Monte Carlo, where we could recharge on the beach during the day before the next sleepless night. Leo was full of energy and very mobile, and friends of ours, especially those in sport, joked that you could already tell he'd be a real athlete.

Patricia's children, Kasper and Bianca, were still little, while Robin was living his own life in Vetlanda. So much was going on in Sweden that it felt natural to leave Monte Carlo for good and move home. For a while, we kept going down to the apartment during school breaks, and we probably became the family that visited the Monaco zoo more than anyone else. We basically lived there during holidays, except for the part of the park that had the snake exhibit. I wouldn't set foot in there. The family always teased me for not going in with them, but I'm so terrified of snakes I can't even look at them behind glass.

We kept travelling a lot, and I kept playing tennis even after Leo was born. He always came along, and early on he developed a big fascination with aircraft, which was convenient, given all the time we spent around them. He was still small when I played an exhibition tournament in Dubai. At that time, the Emirates weren't as developed as they are now, none of those spectacular buildings stretching out into the sea had been built yet. One day we got the chance to take a boat to a small island where new properties were being sold. Once we arrived, they told us we weren't allowed to swim and should be very careful where we stepped. All the sand had been brought in from the desert, and with it came a ton of snakes. Needless to say, we didn't go swimming much on that trip.

But we had a good time anyway. One thing that gave us a lot of laughs was that Leo started calling Mansour Bahrami 'Dad'. We spent a lot of time with Mansour and his wife, and for Leo, he probably felt like a safe presence. But we looked nothing alike – Mansour with his moustache and dark hair – so probably more than a few people must've been confused when Leo shouted 'Daddy!' in his direction.

My friend Mansour was born in Iran, and already in 1977, when the country was still ruled by the Shah, I'd actually gone there to play an ATP tournament. The prize money there was among the biggest outside the Grand Slams, so a lot of top players showed up. The 1979 revolution changed everything. The new regime, with Ayatollah Khomeini as leader, put an end to the tournament.

When I returned in 2004, everything was very different. I remember walking down to the hotel reception in just a T-shirt and shorts. Suddenly, several guards came running and told me to go back to my room and put on long sleeves and trousers. We weren't allowed to undress until we were actually on the tennis court. This was the same club where I'd played the ATP event back in '77. Now, the spectators were separated into male and female sections, and all the women were forced to sit in the sun. I felt sorry for them because it was so hot, and they were completely covered.

When tennis was banned by the regime, along with many other things seen as capitalist or Western, Mansour had to train in secret. He'd practise in an empty swimming pool, and that's how he learned all his trick shots. I don't think anyone in the world is as gifted at that kind of play as he is. His wrists are phenomenal, he can do anything he wants with a tennis ball. I'd probably call him a ball genius, maybe even the best there's ever been.

Eventually, he got out of Iran and settled in France, where he still lives with his family.

When Leo was little, our travels often included fancy dinners and events that weren't always very kid-friendly. People would offer to help with childcare, but we never used babysitters or hired anyone to take care of our kids – or our homes, for that matter. It also came in handy to use Leo as an excuse to leave early.

Just like when Robin was young, my parents were incredibly

helpful. They were always there, first for Robin, then for Patricia's kids Bianca and Kasper, and finally for Leo. Bianca and Kasper split their time with us at our Strandvägen apartment, which we still used as our base. But both Patricia and I felt that the rooms carried too much bad energy from my previous life and past relationships. As glamorous as Strandvägen was, it wasn't a place I felt at home, same as I'd felt on Long Island or in Los Angeles. Too many broken memories.

So we decided to move out to the countryside, to the guesthouse at Alstaholm, where my parents were already living. The place was spacious and beautifully located, complete with a tennis court and a pool. It was a dream place to raise kids, but it also meant lots of long car rides across Stockholm to get the children to school every morning. We had to leave early to make it, and then do it all over again in the afternoon.

For a long time, my parents had had their eye on the house next to Alstaholm. It had a large plot of land and included a big stretch of the bay, so it was very private. They had bought it years earlier but hadn't done anything with it. Now it made sense to set up something more suitable, especially as Dad's health was deteriorating and stairs had become difficult for him.

They renovated the house and turned it into a spacious one-storey villa. That allowed Patricia and me, with our now larger family, to take over Alstaholm itself. The turn-of-the-century house was something special, or maybe it was just us who were sensitive to that kind of thing. A lot of strange, supernatural things happened there. Dishes falling out of cabinets, the feeling of someone being in the room. Sometimes it felt like ancestors, ours or someone else's, were present. Some were friendly, others kind of grumpy. I definitely believe in the supernatural. Spirits linger. My grandmother once promised she'd come back after she passed, but she and my mum made a deal that she'd always knock before entering a room. There have been many times when there's been a knock on the door and no one outside, only for Grandma Greta to have already drifted in. It's never menacing, she just wants to check that everything's okay with me.

Living next door to my parents had its pros and cons, but mostly pros. Mum and Leo became very close, just like she and Dad had always been with Robin. It was like Robin was her own child. Sometimes Patricia found it a bit overwhelming, living like a big extended family. Every now and then we'd come home from a trip to find the whole house rearranged. Mum had moved things around to suit her own taste.

Down in the basement of my parents' house is where Leo and Mum spent a lot of time, and I think that's where his interest in tennis really started. They'd rally against the wall or with each other, just like I used to do against the garage door in Södertälje. Dad even got a little jealous of all the time Leo spent with Mum. One day, when I picked Leo up from preschool, the staff told me he had fallen off a climbing frame. Nothing unusual, he was an active kid. When we got home, he ran to Grandma to play tennis again, but she noticed he was hitting the ball strangely. The next day, he complained that his arm hurt. We went to the hospital. The doctor didn't think it was serious since he could still play tennis. But the X-ray showed that both bones in his right arm, the ones he played with, were broken. They'd never seen a kid with such a high pain tolerance.

My dad eventually had a lifelong wish fulfilled. Dad had dreamed since childhood of having a golden retriever, and when we had the chance to buy a puppy, he was thrilled. The beloved dog, named Lipton, ran between the two houses, and as a true golden retriever, he was usually nearby whenever there was food. But he also ran away a few times, and we'd have to drive around the neighbourhood looking for him. Once we found him at a kids' birthday party a kilometre away, another time in a stable. I'd always have to apologise, but people loved him and often asked if they could keep him for a few more hours. He lived almost thirteen years, and had the dream life every dog deserves.

I was still playing and travelling a lot. Patricia had stopped working entirely – our travels and the demands of raising small children just weren't compatible with her job. It made life easier for me, I won't deny that, and she seemed happy with it too.

Leo loved sport just as much as I did when I was a kid. Besides tennis, he also played floorball – or *innebandy*, a Swedish version of hockey – and football. He was even recruited to join a special development programme at Djurgården, one of Stockholm's biggest football clubs. It was the first time they were investing in players that young, forming a so-called academy. I was thrilled, thinking it was great that he had chosen something other than tennis. But Leo didn't want to let go of tennis entirely, and that meant he wasn't always selected for the football matches.

One night, he couldn't have been more than eight or nine, he called a family meeting. He wanted to tell us something important. As seriously as could be, he announced that from now on, he was going to focus solely on tennis. Patricia cried. And I thought to myself, 'Damn it.'

Of course, we understood him. But we also didn't want him to feel pressured or to be defined entirely by my sport and my life. Just by having the same last name, he was bound to be compared to me. Still, we quickly came to terms with his decision and were impressed that he had the courage to tell us, and that he'd made the decision completely on his own. I've always supported my children in whatever they wanted to pursue, and I did that this time too.

As Leo got older, he often chose to stay at home when I travelled for my own tennis events. He stayed with Grandma and could also travel for his own tournaments. I don't know how many matches my mum has been to as a spectator. He did well, and eventually, Sweden wasn't enough, he started competing internationally. They both loved it.

This was the start of a new life for me, as a travelling tennis dad. I doubt there's ever been a former world number one who's done the same, but I really enjoy being part of Leo's tennis journey. People often ask if we're similar as players. But Leo is definitely more aggressive in his style than I ever was. I had more patience, on the court and in life. But everything moved slower back in my day. Leo's endless practising in the basement with Grandma shows he has the motivation, the true heart of a tennis player. He's independent of me and needs to find his own style and path in tennis. And his temperament is definitely more Fire than Ice, let's put it that way.

Still, there are some similarities. Today, Leo lives in the same building as we do, even the same stairwell. Just like Patricia and I lived next to my parents at Alstaholm. And just like I lived next to mine in the studio apartment in Monte Carlo. He's also extremely particular about food and sleep. And now he has a lovely girlfriend who travels with him to tournaments and is with him through thick and thin.

We go along when we can, but I often find it frustrating to watch, because I can't control anything that happens on the court. He has his own team, and I stay out of it. Maybe I give him the occasional piece of advice, but that's it. People often ask if I'd like to coach a new tennis talent, but I've always said no. I've lived tennis for so many years, and I feel done with it in that sense.

Leo has inherited some of my superstitions, too. We always

have to sit in the exact same seats in the stands, and no one is allowed to move during a match. That's tough for Patricia, who likes to walk around when she's nervous. In fact, she gets so anxious during matches that she almost throws up. Still, Leo puts his foot down. If one of us would have to go to the restroom during a match, that wouldn't be okay. It we did, we'd definitely hear about it afterwards.

When we're at home, we follow his matches live on our phones – usually not with video, just the score, point by point. I don't need to see the screen to understand what's going on, I can read the match just from the score. Patricia can't handle following along on her cell phone, even though she wants to, but she always knows how it's going by looking at me. I get nervous too, of course, but as usual, I don't show it.

My father's health admittedly declined, but when he passed away during Easter 2008, it felt like a punch to the gut. Like the air had been knocked out of me. It was as if his heart just couldn't keep pumping any more. In the final weeks, he was often swollen and only allowed a limited amount of fluids each day. But he was able to stay at home and never needed to be admitted to the hospital, which he always hated.

That Easter, Patricia's parents were visiting, and we were planning to celebrate the holiday together. On Easter Saturday, we were all gathered at the main house, and Dad came over with plastic bags over his feet instead of shoes because of the swelling. But otherwise, he was cheerful and eager to celebrate with his children and grandchildren.

On Easter Sunday, Mum made a lovely lunch. Everyone ate and drank and enjoyed themselves. After the meal, Dad said he felt a bit tired, and like me, he usually liked to take a nap after eating. The rest of us stayed at the table, talking and playing games. After a while, Mum looked at the clock and said: 'Hasn't he been asleep for a really long time? I'd better check on him.'

She went to his room but came running back out, screaming: 'I think Rune is dead!'

Patricia immediately got the defibrillator we had bought for emergencies while we called the ambulance. When all the electrodes were attached properly, the machine just repeated: 'Continue CPR. Continue CPR.'

We knew instinctively that there was nothing to be done. He was already gone. And in a way, maybe it was his time. Just before he lay down, he had walked around the table, hugged each of us and said goodbye. At the time, we didn't think anything of it, we just laughed it off. 'You're not getting rid of us that easily! We'll be here when you wake up!' But he definitely knew what was coming.

It hurts so much to lose someone you love. And this was my father, my rock. I wasn't used to losing people close to me – besides my grandparents on my mother's side, it was the first time for me since the shock of Vitas's passing. It was not long afterwards that I would suffer another huge loss, when Labbe passed away later that same year. But I didn't know that yet.

After we lost Dad, I tried to support Mum. She hadn't been prepared for the worst either. It wasn't easy. My parents had met when they were young and had just celebrated their golden wedding anniversary, fifty years of marriage. Still, Dad died far too soon, at only seventy-six. But he had lived a full life. He got to see me achieve my dreams. I think of him almost every day, and sometimes it reminds me that I won't live for ever either.

But I hope that's still a long way off. Like a cat with nine lives, I've come close to death, almost toyed with it, on more than one occasion. Now I truly want to make the most of my time.

32

Two Champions Meet Again

My own tennis is completely in the past now – I don't play at all any more – but my interest in the game remains. These days, it's just fun to look back, though that certainly wasn't how it felt when I first quit professional tennis. The disappointment was huge, and the fans weren't happy either. They wanted more matches, more excitement, more of the rivalry between us players. John McEnroe wanted that too. He was frustrated that I had quit so abruptly and that he wouldn't get another chance to face me.

Today, I have a good relationship with most of the players from back then. Partly thanks to Patricia, who keeps track of that sort of thing, but even more because of Leo and his success on the tennis tour. I run into many of them again, as a lot are still involved in tennis: some own tournaments, others are tournament directors or heads of their national tennis associations.

When I look back on my career, I'm of course proud of what I accomplished. There are three wins that stand out above all the others in my tennis life. The first is the final against Manuel Orantes in Paris in 1974, where I won my first Grand Slam title. Then, of course, the legendary Wimbledon final against John McEnroe in 1980 – hard to top that. And the third is when our team won Sweden's first-ever Davis Cup title in 1975 against then-Czechoslovakia, at home in the Royal Tennis Hall in Stockholm.

But the best match I've ever played might actually have been a semi-final in Barcelona in 1977 against Eddie Dibbs. At his peak, he was ranked fifth in the world, a truly top-level player. In that match, I led 6–0, 6–0, 3–0, I was playing absolutely flawlessly. I eventually won 6–4 in the third set, after losing a bit of focus, but the level of play was incredible. You play like you're in a trance, everything just works.

When John McEnroe and I see each other these days, we rarely talk about our matches. What's done is done. We made tennis history, sure, but that wasn't something we thought about back then, and it's not something we dwell on now. That said, when we both played on the senior tour, that old rivalry came roaring back. Then it wasn't just for fun, it was win or lose, no in-between. I think it's just in our DNA.

These days, we've both long since found our soulmates, and funnily enough, both of them are named Patricia. I was John's best man at his wedding in 1997 in Hawaii, where I brought Robin along too. John's Patty is a musician and singer, and like us, they're a blended family with kids from previous relationships, now living together as a big modern family. It works well. John and I can finally relax and enjoy the moment.

When we meet up now, it's usually with our families, and they don't have a ton of patience for us going on about the old days. So we mostly talk about life in general. Neither of us is particularly nostalgic; we're just grateful for everything tennis has given us. We've shared so many experiences and it's given us financial security – we're content with that.

After my own father passed away, John's dad became important to me. He was a lawyer in New York, and we really liked each other. Once, John brought him to a senior tournament in Bruges, Belgium. John didn't always have time to keep him company, so his dad John Sr. turned to me and said, very directly: 'Now you take care of me.' So we had a great connection. He knew I had his back. Family ties have always meant a lot to me, and I liked having the old man around.

Until very recently, I was the captain of Team Europe in the Laver Cup, without a doubt the most fun role I've had to take on in my post-tennis life. Partly because I got to spend time with today's tennis stars, hanging out with them for a full week, and partly because I got to feel that competitive edge again, the hunger to win. Team Europe had a strong record, and I hope that continues.

It all started for me in 2016 when Roger Federer and his agent Tony Godsick called me. They had ideas for a brand-new tournament format that was just starting to take shape. They wanted to create a team event in tennis, like golf's Ryder Cup. The concept was Team Europe versus Team World. Golf and tennis are mostly individual sports, so it's fun now and then to compete as a team. Otherwise, there's only the Davis Cup and the United Cup, which are more about national teams.

I remember that call clearly. I was sitting in the sun in Ibiza when they rang, and I was quick to say yes. I haven't regretted it for a second. The format is perfect. It's played over three days, and each match win earns points; the later in the tournament, the more points a win is worth. There are three singles matches and one doubles each day, and the escalating points system keeps things exciting to the very end.

The two teams are kept completely separate and we usually didn't even stay at the same hotels. We ate at different restaurants and only saw each other at press conferences, the opening ceremony and the gala dinner. That created a great atmosphere and a real desire to win. During those game days, I spent all my time with the team. I just wanted to sit and listen to the chatter, all the stuff I remembered so well from my own playing days. And all they wanted was for me to tell stories, memories from the past.

Being captain kept me up to date with the tennis world. I had to pick the best team each year, six players and one substitute, which was incredibly difficult. There were so many good players to choose from, I could've easily picked twenty who were just as strong. But once the team was selected, it was a blast coaching them. It's honestly one of the most fun things I've ever done. The matches were intense, and my job was to motivate them. The playing part they already had down.

It became even more serious when John McEnroe signed on as captain of Team World. Two stubborn competitors facing off again, this time as coaches. The whole setup and drama of the Laver Cup leaned into our historic rivalry. It gave the tournament a nostalgic aura that really worked.

By my side during all those years was Thomas Enqvist as vice-captain. We complemented each other well and had a great partnership. He handled practice schedules and logistics, while I did more press, often alongside the ever-charming John. John's vice captain was his younger brother Patrick, also a very good tennis player, and someone I know well. At our joint press conferences, John did most of the talking, probably 75 per cent of it. I was grateful for that. Just like in the old days, I still get nervous in those situations. When I see today's young stars speaking so easily after matches, I'm impressed. I could never do that, and I never learned how.

One time I even tried my hand at commentating for NBC in the US, which ended up being pretty comical. I was supposed to cover the French Open and then the 1983 Wimbledon final between McEnroe and Chris Lewis. But I barely said a word. Viewers actually called the network asking if I was even there.

My co-commentators were baffled. 'You have to say something,' they told me.

'What should I say? John's obviously going to win.'

Unfortunately, that went out live on air. Turns out, commentating wasn't my thing, especially not when I already knew how the match would go. Plus, we had to be on-site all day. I couldn't handle it. 'Never again', I thought.

We had seven great years with the Laver Cup, and to John's annoyance, Team Europe won five of them. In the autumn of 2024, we both decided to step down as captains after the tournament in Berlin. Yannick Noah and Andre Agassi have taken over as captains now. John and I are both proud of what we built, that we helped create and grow this unique tournament.

People often ask what I do all day now that I've reached a 'normal' retirement age. One of my roles is as an ambassador for Rolex, which means I attend various events they organise around the world. These can include Formula 1 races, equestrian events, sailing, golf, even opera. We ambassadors are like a little family, and we know each other well. From Sweden, it's just me and Stefan Edberg, but many other former tennis players from around the world are also part of the group. We meet at events and enjoy long lunches with interesting people, from film directors to royalty. There's always someone who likes to talk about themselves, and I'm happy to just sit back and listen. Maybe throw in a joke here and there, I do like to laugh and have fun.

The 'Rolex family' has become special to me, especially because Bertrand Gros was chairman for many years. He's one of the most respected lawyers around and worked with major Swiss watch brands and athletes alike. He's the one who used to drag me out of Geneva nightclubs in 1981, when I just wanted to keep partying like there was no tomorrow. He had my best interests at heart, even back then, and that kind of care really sums up the Rolex family. Plus, Rolex was a key sponsor of the Laver Cup while I was involved.

I also still work with Fila. They've been one of my longest-standing sponsors, and some of the people there have been around since my playing days. We're all equally loyal to the brand, and I'm proud to wear their tennis gear. There are plenty of photos of me in Fila gear, some of them have even become iconic. It's the only clothing brand I'd ever consider promoting today. It's become synonymous with me.

When it comes to this kind of business, I'm lucky to have a trusted advisor in Monte Carlo who helps with my investments. I may be good at making money, but I've learned I'm just as good at losing it. After my earlier failures in the business world, I've stayed away from that scene. Fairly soon after the chaos with my companies in the '80s and '90s, I returned to my former partners at IMG. They'd always been in the background, and now I was home again. It was such a relief to be free of all those business types and their constant bullshit. IMG were professionals, and they always kept their word.

What happened with the underwear side of my brand was that Anders Arnborger and Lollo Abrahamsson (then Hildebeck) bought it out of bankruptcy in 1989. I'm still incredibly grateful to them. They did an amazing job with Björn Borg Underwear and quickly built it up to new heights. I'd known them since the days of Björn Borg Design Group, and they saw the potential – that my name was associated with a lot of good things, not just the bad. The shoe and perfume licences also survived thanks to strong products and capable, reliable people.

Lollo and Anders ran Björn Borg Underwear until 2004, when they sold it to venture capitalists with bigger ambitions, like taking the company public. The underwear is now sold almost everywhere in the world. I'm reminded of that often, like when little boys run up and proudly show off their waistband. It's funny that people associate me more with underwear than with tennis. I've never regretted selling the rights to my name. It was a way to restore its reputation after a rough start and having the wrong people involved. That's all in the past now, and I can once again feel proud of my name.

The same year I sold my naming rights, I also had the idea of selling my Wimbledon trophies. It wasn't about needing more money, it was rather about clearing out everything from my old life.

The rest of the family didn't support the idea at all. Patricia has always wanted to preserve the memories from my career to one day pass them on to the kids. Still, in 2006, I went ahead and contacted Bonhams, the well-known auction house in London, and they took on the job very seriously. They got as far as cataloguing the trophies, but that's where it stopped. The auction never happened, because I changed my mind. But that decision came at a price. I had to buy back all my own trophies, and it wasn't cheap.

It was actually John who in the end convinced me to cancel the sale, thank goodness. He called and we talked for a long time about the memories and the hard work behind those five trophies. I'm not a sentimental guy, and that can lead to situations like this, where I don't think things all the way through. Then again, I am quite stubborn.

My mum saved everything: newspaper clippings, trophies, rackets, clothes. I had nothing left myself. Most of it went to charity or was left behind in hotel rooms. What was later left after Mum passed away ended up at the Swedish Sports Museum. As for the famous garage door, I honestly don't know where it is. When the house on Torekällgatan was renovated, they took it down, and for years it was stored by the local municipality. The idea was to eventually house it in a Björn Borg museum, which they had big plans for. But something must have happened and the idea fizzled out. And the door? Last I heard, it was featured in some TV auction show.

33

Family Secrets

I was an only child and a bit of a lone wolf. Maybe it's no surprise that my dad ended up being my best friend – he had cut ties with his own family early on and had only vague connections to the past. My mum was an only child too, and so is Patricia. So we actually have a lot in common. We've all learned to take care of each other, to look after the family we've got.

My parents didn't have many friends outside the family circle. Of course, some people tried to latch on once I became famous, but my parents chose to be with each other, and with me. And I've grown into the same kind of person.

The reason my dad broke ties with his family was that my grandfather remarried – a woman my dad didn't like and who didn't treat him well. There was no real motherly love, and it seems she drove a wedge between him and his father. My grandfather worked in the clothing business and travelled a lot. That meant my dad, Rune, had to stay home with his stepmother, and of course he missed his father terribly the whole time. When his dad came home, Rune was overjoyed. Maybe that's why my dad also got into the clothing business at an early age.

Dad told me that he neither wanted to nor was allowed to visit the home that later existed on Götgatan in Stockholm. Still, once or twice when I was little, he took me there to meet my grandfather.

I remember we played cards for money, one-krona coins, and my pockets were so full when we left, they jingled with every step. I guess I was already a born competitor. Years later, when I'd made a name for myself in tennis, Dad's family tried to reconnect. But it just felt fake. If they hadn't cared before, why should we suddenly start hanging out now?

I don't remember much about the woman who lived with my grandfather. She was 'Grandma' to me at the time, but I only saw my grandfather maybe ten times in my life. Since Dad didn't see him much, I really didn't get anything from that side of the family. Instead, we spent all our time with my mum's parents, Grandma Greta and Grandpa Martin. They were part of that little triangle: Mum, Dad and me.

As for my real grandmother, I had no idea what happened to her. We never talked about her, and I think we all just assumed she'd passed away. It wasn't until very recently, while working on this book, that the truth came out. I had actually had a grandmother all along. She'd been living close by the whole time, down in Skärholmen, not far from Södertälje and Fruängen, where my other grandparents lived and where I visited often.

Her name was Linnea, and from what I know, she never got to meet me. She disappeared from my grandfather's life, but continued living on quietly in Skärholmen until old age. It really broke my heart to find this out so late. Just the thought that she had been there all those years without us ever meeting.

She knew I was her grandson, but I had no idea she existed. Maybe she even watched me play on TV. I just hope she had a good life.

My dad Rune was her only child. Why didn't I ever ask him more about this? Did he miss her? What had really happened between them? I was probably just too caught up in my own life. It feels strange not to have known this, especially since our family has always been so close. But tough topics were never really discussed. I remember once seeing my dad sitting at the kitchen table at Alstaholm, lost in thought. I asked him, 'Is something bothering you?'

He told me that he had recently found out his half-brother Roffe had died, and that the funeral was being held that very day. When he said Roffe's name, I remembered him from my childhood. He used to be at Grandma and Grandpa's house on Resarö, and I always had so much fun when he let me shoot his air rifle or when I played tennis with him. That was actually Dad's idea, and I won easily, even though I was only seven or eight years old. After that, Roffe never played tennis again.

But the best thing about Roffe was that he loved speedboats, and my absolute favourite thing was to go out with him in his racing boat that did twenty-five knots. That's probably where my love of fast boats comes from. I could see how much Dad was hurting over Roffe's death and how hard it was for him not having had any contact with his family for so long. So I said to him, 'Put on something nice. We're going to the funeral!'

When we walked into the church, we were definitely met with some surprised faces. As I recall, Roffe died of cancer, far too young. I still believe Dad's family followed my career and knew what I was up to. It was just one of those things, bad timing, missed connections.

*

After that brutal year in 2008, when both my dad and Labbe passed away just a few months apart, we felt like the family needed something to hold us together. So we took my mum and went on a vacation to South Africa, the whole family. We needed to get away, spend time together and create new memories to build on.

One early morning, we took a boat out to Robben Island off the coast of Cape Town to see where Nelson Mandela had been imprisoned. The boat ride itself was beautiful, and being on the island really put things into perspective. I thought back to the time I'd met Mandela in person, years earlier. It was a special moment to share with my family and gave me a chance to tell them about that experience.

But more than anything, I needed a mental break after that tough year. People say grief gets easier with time, and I guess that's true to some extent, especially if you stay active and keep your mind busy. But if I'm alone with my thoughts for too long, I easily slide into a dark place. That's how it was then. Losing both Dad and Labbe hit me really hard. I felt like I'd lost my footing completely.

Luckily, our family doesn't sit still for long, and Leo's tennis gave me something else to focus on. In the coming years, we drove all over Sweden for different junior tournaments. I ended up seeing more of the country than I ever did as a so-called tourism ambassador. We kept travelling internationally too – back to South Africa a few more times, and also to places like the Seychelles, Mauritius and Vietnam. But once we got home, it was straight back to the grind: traffic jams, homework and endless hours of training. For me, the best part of travelling has always been escaping everyday life for a while. And slowly, with time, those deep wounds started to heal, even for my mum.

*

My mother was a special woman, an incredibly strong presence. While my dad, Rune, was the glue that held us together, my mum was the one who ran the show. She was dominant, larger than life and made the decisions. When it came to business, she could be tough, and she was the one who managed all of that over the years: dealing with banks, investors, contracts and business deals. She always wanted to protect me and had my best interests at heart, but sometimes it got a bit out of hand. Even after I met Patricia, she didn't really want to let go. In a way, I get it, considering everything that had happened in my past relationships, but it was still hard for Patricia to feel that my mum saw her as some kind of gold digger. On top of that, we were living practically next door, and at times it felt suffocating, though overall it was mostly positive, especially for the kids.

With a will as strong as my mother's, there were definitely some fiery clashes between us. I could get incredibly angry with her. Sometimes it was about things from long ago, like the time she lost me – or maybe let me wander off – and I ended up at the police station. Or how stressful it was for me when she worked providing daycare and there were always other kids at our house. I confronted her about those things, and the strange thing was, she never pushed back.

It was always her approval I craved, like when I brought home my very first trophy. At the same time, I know life hadn't been easy for her. She grieved not having more children. Maybe that's why she clung so tightly to Robin, sometimes almost like she was taking him over from us. But she was also a great source of comfort for him, and I probably had myself to blame because I was often so far away. My parents were able to give my son the stability he needed.

*

Once the kids had grown up and moved out, we felt done with country life and decided to move back into the city. It was a huge upgrade in quality of life. Not spending hours in the car any more made me wonder why we hadn't done it sooner.

The main reason, of course, was that Mum lived next door, and her health had started to decline. It just felt wrong to leave her behind. She had become so lonely, and it was hard for her to rebuild her life after Dad died. We always tried to include her in whatever we were doing. It was almost like she became a part of our marriage.

After Patricia and I got married for the second time, in Las Vegas, we continued on to Los Angeles. While we were there, we decided to visit a medium. We were curious, open to what it might bring, and since we both have an interest in the supernatural, we thought it would be interesting to hear a medium's take on our future together. Several of us in the family have a spiritual side, like being able to sense when something's about to happen. That's especially true for Leo, while Robin is more down-to-earth and practical. But even Robin could feel something strange sometimes, like the house at Alstaholm being haunted.

The female medium we met emphasised that we shouldn't keep living so close to my mum, or even in that house at all. She saw that it was draining us, and that the energy around us wasn't good. She even offered to cleanse the house of bad spirits over the phone. We politely declined that unusual offer. In Los Angeles, mediums are big business, run like any other company, complete with card readers at the front desk. But clearing bad energy over the phone? That was a step too far for us.

Still, what the medium said planted a seed in my mind. We needed to do something to reclaim time for ourselves. And she was right about everything. I didn't want anything, not even my own mother, to come between me and Patricia.

My mum had one last wish in life: to see Leo play at Wimbledon. And she did, tears of joy in her eyes, when he played in junior Wimbledon in 2019. On 15 February 2021, she took her last breath. The day before, Valentine's Day, I had gone out to Alstaholm to visit her. She was never one for celebrations, but I'm so grateful I got to see her that day. She fought until the end, never had to go to the hospital, and was able to pass away at home.

Robin took her death very hard, just like when my dad died. To him, they'd been like his parents, and the grief hit hard. Leo was in South America at the time, playing a tournament in Paraguay. He usually talked to his grandma every day, but I didn't want to break the news to him over the phone when he was so far away. We decided we'd meet him in person at his next tournament and tell him then. This was during the pandemic, so we had to take all the tests and then fly to Paris to catch a connecting flight to Rio de Janeiro. One more flight later, we arrived in Porto Alegre in southern Brazil, where Leo was playing. We met him at the hotel, and strangely, he didn't ask many questions. 'We'll tell him about his grandma as soon as he's out of the tournament,' I told Patricia.

He won his first match, and we looked at each other. 'Tomorrow we'll tell him!'

But he kept winning, match after match. In the end, he won the entire tournament, one of the biggest and most prestigious junior tournaments in the world, and I was incredibly proud and happy for him.

After the final, we sat down with him and told him about his grandmother. He said he already knew, he had felt her with him during the matches. There had been a little butterfly fluttering around Patricia and me in the stands the whole time. It lingered for a long while and for us, it was obvious: that was Margareta, still with us in spirit, even after death.

When we came home and started sorting everything out, we realised she had hardly left anything behind. The house had already been cleared out, like she had orchestrated the whole thing before she passed. She'd had help from a couple of acquaintances who lived nearby and often helped her with practical things like shovelling snow. The whole thing felt very strange. And then, just days after she passed, those acquaintances moved away too. All that was left in the house was a worn-out old couch and some Wimbledon trophies tossed into a bag. It's not the big trophy you see at the award ceremony. That one stays at the club.

Most likely, Mum had arranged with that couple in advance how everything would be handled after her death. To signal she was still alive, she was supposed to send them a thumbs-up emoji every morning. The day no message came, they'd know to set the plan in motion. It was all so strange, and I couldn't grieve properly because I didn't understand why she had done it this way. Maybe she just wanted to spare us the hassle of dealing with things after she was gone.

Both my parents had wished to be cremated and have their ashes scattered at sea, where they could be reunited. We've never been religious or churchgoers in my family, so we never had traditional funerals or graves. My maternal grandparents are in a memorial garden in Gustavsberg, but it's not a place we visit often. They're with us anyway. The memories live inside me, not on a headstone. That's always felt natural to me, even though Patricia and I have now agreed to have a shared burial plot. It feels like I owe that much to the Swedish people.

34

At Last

Patricia set firm boundaries from the very beginning. There were certain people we just couldn't be around, because she knew it could drag me into the wrong crowd and bad habits. Because of that, she's sometimes got a bit of a reputation as the 'boring' one, the one who's held me back, watched over me. There have been times she's literally dragged me home when things got out of hand and started heading in the wrong direction. She's done it to protect me, to make sure I survived, and I honestly have her to thank for still being alive. Having her by my side gives me an incredible sense of security.

We pretty much do everything together, and I think she's got a bit of my mother in her, that same kind of grit and fierce determination that I seem to need. In a way, she's also my guardian angel. I've felt the presence of a guardian angel more than once in my life, like all those times I've been close to death, in the air, in deep water, or because of drugs. These days I have a guardian angel tattooed on my arm, and so does Patricia. It was my first tattoo, and I remember my mum wasn't thrilled about it. She immediately blamed Patricia. She also asked why I'd want a little bird on my arm. Later on, I got another tattoo: a bear dad with two cubs, Robin and Leo, of course.

Besides relying on fate or guardian angels, I do what I can to maintain self-control in my life. One of my biggest things is exercise. If I don't get to move every day, I feel like I'll go crazy. I can't calm down. I walk, I bike, I need to get my heart rate up to quiet my nerves. Back in my tennis days, we didn't really do strength training, so I still mostly focus on cardio. I do some of my best thinking on the bike. The shower, though, is different. That's where I start overthinking, and sometimes I walk out furious about something I just realised in there. Patricia sometimes even warns me before I step in. She knows what might happen.

I don't really like being around people, but I've figured out how to train just fine at home. I spend about 45 minutes in front of the TV, then it's straight into the shower. At that point, I feel satisfied, like I've actually done something with my day. After that, I usually settle into the couch and take a breather. But I still need to hit my daily step goal, and I do that by walking around the apartment. I just pace back and forth around the TV couch until I've hit my 20 kilometres on the pedometer. Patricia can get really annoyed when she's trying to relax with me and I suddenly get up and start walking. Believe me when I say there are tracks worn into the floor around our sofa.

Self-discipline runs deep in me. Despite how controlled I seem on the outside, there's a rollercoaster going on inside. My way of managing life is to keep things strict: sleep, food, exercise. But I only apply those standards to myself, I rarely comment on anyone else's habits.

I'm a bit of an 'all or nothing' person. Sometimes, I'll really indulge if I go out, especially if there's alcohol. But hard liquor and red wine don't work for me any more. I stick to white wine or beer now. The whole thing with gourmet food and indulgence came after my career. I had lived under such pressure and control for so long that once I stopped playing tennis, everything just flipped. I completely lost control and started devouring everything. When I let go, it feels like such a relief, but it easily turns into overdoing it. If that happens, I have to slam on the brakes, actually more like the emergency brake, followed by a period of self-punishment. At home, that means even more time on the bike and living almost like a monk.

To this day, I still struggle with feeling awkward when it comes to talking and socialising. Sure, I can be social when needed, I've travelled the world, met people constantly, and I learned to manage that at fifteen. But I'm happiest at home, with my family around me. Honestly, I don't want to leave the house unless I absolutely have to.

Every morning I calibrate the scale before I weigh myself. It might sound a little obsessive, I even put dumbbells on it to make sure it's spot-on. Not even 100 grams off. I've always done things like this, though it's not something I've ever told anyone. I'm sure the other tennis players had their own rituals too.

Even after all that weighing, I might still go downstairs and scarf down a bunch of cheese and ham sandwiches, which I love. Best of all is if we've got liver pâté and pickled cucumber, those are must-haves. The only problem is Patricia thinks the pâté is disgusting and doesn't even want it in the fridge. Still, I take pride in not gaining weight. These days I weigh exactly the same as I did when I was active, though back then, I had a lot more muscle.

My sense of balance has always been bad, so bad, in fact, that

I don't get seasick or carsick. People are often surprised I could play world-class tennis with that kind of balance, but clearly, it worked out. I was also incredibly stiff, despite Labbe's constant massages. Today's top players are way more flexible. Take someone like Novak Djokovic, he moves like a gymnast. Flexibility is way more important in tennis today, which is why so many players do yoga.

I try to combat my stiffness with exercise and massage. The problem is, after all these years, I find massage incredibly boring. So I don't do it as regularly as I probably should. Unfortunately, I can't massage myself, but I learned a lot from Labbe, and now I'm usually the one massaging both my wife and Leo. I go just as long as Labbe used to. Patricia always tries to cheat and get up early, but I say what Labbe used to: 'Nope, not done yet. Stay put.'

A typical day for me always looks about the same: I'm up at six, then train after a light breakfast. Around eleven or twelve we have lunch, maybe grilled chicken and potatoes, and then I take a nap, sometimes for up to an hour. I really need that nap; it's always helped me feel good. After that, I have coffee and maybe watch a film or documentary. I like true stories or sports docs best.

What really fascinates me, though, is mountain climbing. I know everything about it, every peak, and I've seen every documentary about it that's been shown on TV. I've often dreamed of climbing Mount Everest. There's something about that rush, always pushing forwards and upwards. That drive has always been in me, but I could never actually do it. The last book I read was the autobiography of Swedish climber Göran Kropp. I was hooked. Imagine standing on the top of the world, not to look down, but for the journey it took to get there. That achievement, that path, that's what draws me in. I admire all climbers, but most of all the sherpas. They do unbelievable work.

Sometimes in the afternoon I have to take care of practical things, maybe answer an interview or deal with something related to work. Later, around five, Patricia and I meet up on the couch after she's finished with her own day. We might watch something together or just talk. We don't usually eat a full dinner, just sandwiches. I'm a real sandwich person. I still fall asleep by ten, unless it's a full moon. Then I don't sleep at all. Even at night, my brain's going full speed. I have vivid dreams, and tennis often shows up in them. Sometimes I talk in my sleep or even 'play' tennis in bed so hard that the whole thing shakes. I have to win, even at night.

The seasons affect me a lot. I tend to get really low when autumn comes and the darkness sets in. Looking back, I probably needed some sort of doping just to get through those months during my career. My lowest points were always during the tournaments after September, that's when my mood just dropped. But no one talked much about that back then. These days I'm more aware, and I know that every autumn, a mild depression creeps in. My mind and body, especially after all those years of intense training, start longing for a simpler life, for warmth and sunlight.

It's no surprise that my body's worn down now. I've got practically no cartilage left. I've had multiple knee surgeries. The last one was done by the doctor for the Swedish national hockey team, and he said he'd never seen anything worse. So it's no wonder at all that I'm in pain. One big difference from before is that I can take time off and spend parts of the year in warmer places.

The first time we went to Cape Verde off the coast of Senegal was in 2017. Even on the plane, the crew asked why we were going there: 'There's nothing exciting to do!' they said. That sounded like music to our ears. Peaceful and perfect. The warmth did wonders for body and soul, so we quickly bought a house on the island of Sal. No one cared who I was. Most people didn't know, and those who did left me alone.

At first, Cape Verde was amazing, an oasis in the middle of the Atlantic, with horses running wild on the beach and hardly any tourists. But eventually it got popular, and it became harder for me to be there. I started to feel watched and just wanted to stay inside. That kind of ruined the magic, and in the end, we decided to sell our beloved house. Instead, we found our dream home in Ibiza, where we can still be anonymous. We'll probably spend more time there and less in Sweden. In Ibiza, I can really disconnect. I smell the pine trees and hear the cicadas, just like in my beautiful memories of Cap Ferrat.

Friends visit often. One of them is Boris Becker, who's become a close friend. We've had many long, deep conversations on Ibiza, about tennis and about life. He talks tennis with Leo, too, and I love listening. Boris really challenges him to think and go deeper, which is much needed, and he has a real ability to dig deep. On the island, we can be carefree, just take a boat to a quiet cove, dive into the turquoise water and float. Hear the music and laughter from other boats, toss a ball around and let the waves rock us. Talk about life, laugh until we cry.

It's strange, but lately I've been thinking more and more about things that happened a long time ago. Of all the questions I've been asked in interviews over the years, one keeps popping into my mind. It was about how I'll look back on my life when I'm seventy-five. Will I be able to lean back, reflect, and maybe even feel proud of what I've done? I don't even remember what I answered, just the question.

Back then, seventy-five felt a lifetime away. Now it's not that far off. Life has gone by far too fast. They say it only speeds up with time, and I believe it. These days, I'm more careful with life. I don't want to risk anything any more. I just want to have peace and be able to live.

I'm looking forward to many summers in Ibiza, sitting with a cup of coffee in hand, just gazing out over the water and feeling at peace. When I sit there and reflect on life, I want to finally feel proud, and let that joy fill my body. Everything turned out okay!

35

Heartbeats

Thump-thump, thump-thump, thump-thump . . .
There were my heartbeats again. Like a tennis
ball bouncing off the ground. Slow, just the way
I was used to hearing and feeling them. I was
alive, but I didn't recognise myself at all.

'What happened?' I mumbled.

The memories started to slowly come back, and I realised I was in a hospital. Bare white walls, and in the background, the muffled sounds of people moving around and machines beeping. I could barely open my eyes, I felt so groggy after being under anaesthesia for what had apparently been a three-hour surgery. Everything carried the faint smell of disinfectant. I felt small and helpless in that sterile hospital room, suddenly so exposed, lying there in a thin hospital gown with the open back.

A nurse walked in. She was wearing blue scrubs that looked like they were made of paper, something disposable at the end of the day.

'How are you feeling?' she asked.

A wave of panic hit me. What I really wanted to say was that everything was awful, but as usual I replied, 'I'm fine, thanks.'

Life had been going great. For a long time, I had no idea what was coming. Something had started growing inside me, a silent enemy I couldn't feel and that was hard to detect. Was I not going to be able to keep living?

A few days earlier, I'd been diagnosed with prostate cancer. The doctors had told us that my quality of life would probably decline after surgery, and that maybe I could go on living for a few more years without any issues if I chose not to have the operation. But now, looking back, I realise there never really was a choice, because the cancer turned out to be extremely aggressive. The doctors said I would have died if I hadn't had the surgery. Maybe I had fooled myself into thinking I had a choice. But that's just the mind and the subconscious playing tricks on you. The truth is, I never had a choice.

It's a bit ironic, really, how powerless I had become. I'd always used my body as my main tool, always known exactly what to do to improve my fitness and performance. Now, I couldn't do anything. You can't train cancer away. No one's immune, not even if you stay fit. But at least you have a chance if you get tested. So I definitely want to urge every man who can to do it.

I had been getting bloodwork done regularly, I've always liked keeping tabs on my health. That's how I knew my numbers were climbing. But when things got serious, I didn't even want to do the tests, let alone go through with surgery. It got so bad they eventually had to sedate me just to examine how far the cancer had progressed.

It turned out I was in the most advanced stage. It was hard to take in, especially because I hadn't felt sick at all, not even the slightest symptom.

Now the surgery was done, and I could hear my heartbeat again, steady and calm, just as always. I was lying there in my hospital bed at Sankt Göran's in Stockholm, staring out at the grey January sky. There wasn't even a TV to distract me. At home, Patricia usually puts on a show for me that just keeps rolling on with new episodes. If I doze off, it's comforting to know it'll still be playing, especially if she needs to leave the house. But here in the hospital, she couldn't do that. And I really don't like it when there's total silence, I need some kind of sound around me. My thoughts kept pouring in. My head felt both heavy and light at the same time. Patricia dropped by with some magazines and a treat to eat, but she could only stay for a short while.

There's always a risk the cancer might spread, and that's something I'll have to live with for a while now. Every six months, I'll go through the anxious wait to find out if we caught it in time. The fear comes and goes. But that's life, isn't it? You never really know what's coming. You just have to make the most of each day. Love the people close to you. Watch your kids and grandkids grow up. Kiss your wife every morning.

It could've ended so many times before, with me as my own worst enemy. Now I have a new opponent in cancer, one I can't control. But I'm going to beat it. I'm not giving up. I fight like every day is a Wimbledon final.

And those usually go pretty well, don't they?

Epilogue

I look back on my life with pride. Sure, my career is something most people could only dream of, but what I'm most proud of is my sons. In the same way, I hope they can be proud of me. I've always put a lot of pressure on myself, not just professionally, but also in my private life. That's why I've always wanted to be the best husband I can be, the best father to my children.

It hasn't always gone the way I hoped. The anxiety I feel when things fall apart can be overwhelming. Still, I'm not someone who lives with regrets. Sure, I sometimes wonder: 'What would've happened if I'd acted differently? If I'd made another choice?' But I believe in fate, and that life has brought me exactly where I'm meant to be.

I'm satisfied with what I've accomplished, and that I've pushed myself to see how far I could go, for better or worse. In tennis, that drive took me to the top of the world. In life, it brought me to rock bottom with addiction, and then to the high point where I am today. I love being alive, and I love seeing my children and grandchildren grow into their own people, even if I can still see little pieces of myself in them.

Life is meant to be lived, and today I'm lucky enough to choose where, when and how. In Ibiza, I enjoy the sun and the warmth. I can walk into town, have a coffee or a beer. There's always someone we know who stops by for a quick chat about the weather, plans for the day, or to recommend a new restaurant. They know who I am, but they don't care. Here, I'm just another face in the crowd.

Like Robinson Crusoe, I can sit on my little island, gaze out over the sea and finally feel at peace. My body softens in the light and the heat. Parts of me are a bit worn down, but if there's one thing all of us tennis players agree on, it's this: It was worth it.

All those hours on the court and off it. All the wins, and the losses. The cheers and the tears. The highs and the lows.

I am so grateful.

Acknowledgements

Thank you for picking up this book. We've been working on it nonstop for nearly three years, from the initial idea to publication. It's been a journey filled with both laughter and tears, as memories once buried have come to the surface. From the very start, we said that if we could get through this project without breaking up or falling out, we could get through anything. And we did. It's also a relief to finally share my whole life, even the darker parts.

We want to extend a huge thank you to our publisher, Norstedts, and everyone involved there. It's been a mutual choice from start to finish. The little writing room at the publishing house was put to good use, and honestly we'll be a bit disappointed if they don't rename it 'The Borg Room'. Thank you to our wonderful senior editor, Gunilla, and our line editor, Fredrik. The weather was always terrible when we were scheduled to meet, but we made it to you rain or shine. Thanks to our publisher, Håkan, for your comments and insights. Thank you, Linda, for your tireless work in bringing the book to readers all over the world. And thank you, Sara, for all your help with communications – everything from author photos to interviews. A big thanks to Björn Hellberg for fact-checking all our tennis references. There's truly no one like you when it comes to having every bit of information and trivia in your head. Thank you, Jan Waldekranz, for narrating the audiobook for the Swedish version. You and Björn grew up together and have always kept in touch. It means a lot that it's your voice bringing Björn's story to life.

A very special thanks to our entire family for putting up with us during this time. We know this book project hasn't always been easy for you. You didn't get to choose whether or not to be in the limelight, but you are all amazing, and together we can get through anything. Just like always, it's a family affair.

Patricia and Björn